THE CHAKRAS
&
ESOTERIC HEALING

THE CHAKRAS
&
ESOTERIC HEALING

Zachary F. Lansdowne, Ph.D.

SAMUEL WEISER, INC.

York Beach, Maine

First published in 1986 by
Samuel Weiser, Inc.
Box 612
York Beach, ME 03910

Fifth printing, 1993

Library of Congress Catalog Card Number: 84-51108

ISBN 0-87728-584-5
MG

Printed in the United States of America

The paper used in this publication meets the minimum
requirements of the American National Standard for Perma-
nence of Paper for Printed Library Materials Z39.48-1984.

Contents

List of Tables

Acknowledgments

Appreciation is expressed to the Health Science Press, Essex, England, for permission to reproduce Figure 2: Locations of the Major Etheric Chakras; and to the Theosophical Publishing House, Wheaton, Illinois, for permission to reproduce Figure 3: Man and His Etheric Centres.

Introduction

In traditional yoga philosophy, the chakras are subtle force centers that vitalize and control the physical body. The Sanskrit word *chakra* means "wheel," indicating that these force centers are wheels of energies. The purpose of this book is to explain how various experiences in human consciousness and esoteric healing occur, in terms of the chakras and other aspects of a person's inner constitution.

The subject of consciousness will be examined in several ways. The evolution of consciousness will be traced from the beginning human embryo, to the fetus, and then through the various stages of human experience, where this evolution unfolds according to the sequence of development for the chakras. Meditation and self-hypnosis will be discussed, including their differences and their effects on consciousness. Also described will be how the practice of meditation changes as consciousness evolves. And the differences between spiritual development and psychic opening will be explained.

The following methods of esoteric healing will be examined in detail:

Pranic healing is one of the oldest and most widespread methods of treatment for physical illness. In this approach the healer uses a type of energy that is sometimes called prana, magnetism, or vitality. This energy can be consciously directed by the healer toward the patient, so that the healer's vitality replaces or reinforces that of the patient. The healer uses his chakras to assimilate the prana, convert it into healing energy, and then distribute this energy. The patient's chakras receive the energy, which serves to vitalize his physical body and more especially his endocrine gland system, thereby bringing about physical health.

Telepathic healing can be used either to transmit helpful ideas that may affect the patient's mental attitudes or to guide the patient's subconscious mind for healing his physical body. Several types of telepathic impulses can be sent: intuitional, mental, or emotional. The healer's chakras are used to send these impulses, and the patient's chakras are used to register them.

Radiatory healing can be accomplished when the healer is in alignment with his inner spiritual nature. The qualities resulting from this alignment can be radiated to the patient to calm his emotions, stimulate compassion, strengthen his mind, and bring him into alignment with his own spiritual nature. The healer's chakras radiate these qualities, and the patient's chakras register them.

The approach used by this book is to review and integrate the writings of several authors having a theosophical perspective. While none of these authors gives a complete and unified picture of the entire subject matter, such a picture will be presented by synthesizing the individual contributions. Chapter 1 will briefly define certain terms and relationships regarding the inner constitution of a human being. Chapter 2 will present background material on the chakras, including their functions, locations, and relationships with endocrine glands. Chapter 3 will consider various aspects of consciousness, including meditation, self-hypnosis, spiritual development, and psychic opening. Chapters 4, 5, and 6 will examine pranic, telepathic, and radiatory healing. And Chapter 7 will present conclusions.

Also included are five appendices providing interpretations, in terms of the chakras, of previously published symbolic formulas that heretofore have never been fully explained. Appendices I, II, and III interpret symbols from the writings of Alice A. Bailey; Appendices IV and V interpret symbols from the last book of the Bible, the Revelation of St. John the Divine.

A comprehensive set of notes identifies the sources for the various ideas and statements that are included. These notes will enable the reader to investigate any aspect of the subject matter that is of special interest.

———•———

Chapter 1

Inner Constitution

A fundamental teaching of theosophy is that the solar system is sevenfold in its constitution. Whereas only the physical world can be perceived with the ordinary senses, it is said that there are also six higher worlds, of progressively subtler matter, that interpenetrate the physical. These worlds, called *planes,* have been given definite names. It is also said that a person has a "vehicle of consciousness" or a "body" on all of the planes. This chapter will introduce briefly certain terms and relationships regarding a person's inner constitution as understood by various theosophical writers, with the purpose of providing the background material needed for later chapters on chakras, consciousness, and healing.[1]

Physical Plane

Figure 1 on page 2 illustrates the human constitution according to theosophy. This diagram gives the following names for the seven planes in the solar system: physical, emotional, mental, buddhic, atmic, monadic, and adi; the physical plane is the lowest, and the adi is the highest. Although other terms are sometimes used to designate the seven planes, the foregoing are the names that will be employed in this presentation.

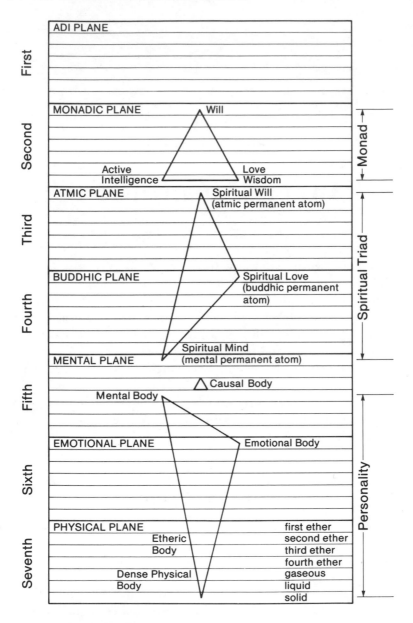

Figure 1. Inner Constitution. This figure illustrates the human constitution according to theosophy. Each of the seven planes is divided into seven subplanes, denoted by the horizontal lines. It is important for the reader to note the placement of the four triangles with respect to the subplanes.

Figure 1 also indicates that each plane is further divided into seven subplanes. For example, the physical is the seventh or lowest plane, and it consists of the following subplanes:

1. First ether
2. Second ether
3. Third ether
4. Fourth ether
5. Gaseous
6. Liquid
7. Solid

The three lowest subplanes—gaseous, liquid, and solid—compose the dense world of matter and are perceptible with the five physical senses. The four highest subplanes represent the etheric region. Although imperceptible with normal faculties, these four ethers nevertheless do consist of matter from the physical realm. Table 1 on page 4 gives the functions of the four etheric subplanes according to several authors.

Corresponding to the division of the physical plane into dense and etheric portions, a person's physical body has two portions:

The dense physical body is composed of solids, liquids, and gases, including such parts as the bones, blood system, nervous system, brain, and endocrine glands.

The etheric body, sometimes called the vital body, is composed of the four ethers. It is referred to in the Bible as the "golden bowl" (Eccles. 12:6).

The etheric body has the following functions: Although of a tenuous nature, it is the framework or foundation underlying every part of the dense physical body; it vitalizes or energizes the dense physical cells; it is a clearinghouse for all forces coming to the physical from higher dimensions, transmitting them through the nervous, endocrine, and blood systems; it is the transmitter and receiver of telepathic impulses of an intuitive, mental, or emotional nature; and it provides the channel for the physically focused consciousness to register the subtler worlds. The etheric body is below the threshold of consciousness and is generally recognized only in terms of vitality or lack of vitality. Its seven major force centers, called chakras, will be considered in Chapter 2.[2]

Table 1. Functions of the Four Physical Plane Ethers, According to Various Sources*

Name	Besant Function	Chaney Function	Saraydarian Function
First ether	Medium for the transmission of thought from brain to brain	"Channel for the transmission of thought from one individual to another"	"It helps in formulating thought-forms. In it are stored all of our memories."
Second ether	Medium of "the finer forms of electricity"	Channel for the "emotional systems of waves" and the kundalini power	"It carries heat and energy to the muscles and the nervous system."
Third ether	Medium of light	Channel for prana emanating from sun	"Produces energies for propagation"
Fourth ether	Medium of ordinary current electricity and of sound	"Channel for all the *physical* forces with which we are familiar including electricity, magnetism, heat, sound, light"	"It carries a certain kind of energy which helps the body assimilate food and grow."

*The functions listed in this table come from the following sources: *Ladder of Lives*, by A. Besant (quoted in Powell's *The Etheric Double*, page 3); "Man—the Measure of All Things," by E.C. Chaney, pages 1-7; and H. Saraydarian's *Cosmos in Man*, page 67. For full publication data, the reader should refer to the title listing in the Bibliography.

The planet also has both a dense physical body and an etheric body. The planetary dense body is the familiar tangible world of sense perceptions. Even though the planetary etheric body is not normally perceptible, it plays a key role in understanding the healing process because it is an important medium for the transmission of energies from the healer to patient. As will be discussed in Chapters 4, 5, and 6, the planetary etheric body can be used as a medium for sending pranic, telepathic, and radiatory energies.

Emotional Plane

The sixth plane illustrated in Figure 1 is the emotional, which also consists of seven subplanes. A person's emotional body is said to be constructed from the matter of all seven subplanes. The emotional body has the following functions:

To make sensation possible. The emotional body converts the vibrations received from the physical plane into sensations, which are then passed on to the mental body (which will be discussed in the next section) where they appear as perceptions. The emotional body can add to a sensation the quality of "pleasant" or "unpleasant," so that it is registered by the mind as a pleasant or unpleasant perception. The emotional body also can give to a sensation any feeling, such as desire, fear, or envy.

To serve as a bridge between mind and physical matter. Conversely, thinking sets in motion mental matter, which causes the emotional body to vibrate, thus affecting etheric matter, which then acts on the dense matter of the physical brain. All thinking requires the coordination of the mental body with the dense physical brain.

To act as an independent vehicle of consciousness and action. There are several ways that this independence could be achieved: During ordinary waking consciousness, the powers of the emotional senses (including clairvoyance and clairaudience) could be brought into action; during sleep or trance, the emotional body can separate itself from the physical and then function independently; and after physical

Table 2. Etheric and Emotional Causes of Physical Disease*

Body	Cause	Description*
Etheric	Congestion	"It is this congestion at the point of intake and of outlet in the etheric body which is responsible for the impeding of the free flow of the life force, with the results of a rapid succumbing to diseases."
	Lack of coordination and integration	"The physical form in its dense aspect is too loosely connected with the etheric form or counterpart. This leads to a devitalised and debilitated condition, which predisposes man to sickness or ill health."
	Overstimulation of the centers	"Every part of the physical body is in a constant condition of stimulation, of galvanic effort, with a resultant activity in the nervous system which—if not correctly regulated—can lead to a great deal of distress."
Emotional	Uncontrolled and ill-regulated emotion	"The tendency to criticism, to violent dislikes, and to hatreds based on criticism or a superiority complex, produces much of the acidity from which the majority of people suffer."
	Inhibited desire	"Where desire is inhibited . . . all kinds of diseases—cancer, congestion of the lungs and certain liver complaints—become possible, as well as the dread malady of tuberculosis."
	Rampant desire	"It should be noted that where desire is rampant and uncontrolled and no inhibition is present, such diseases as the syphilitic disorders, homosexuality and inflammations and fevers appear."
	Fear and worry	"They lower the vitality of the man to such a point that he becomes susceptible to disease. The scourge of influenza has its roots in fear and worry."
	Irritation	"It is interesting to note that certain forms of eye trouble are caused by this."

*The material in this table comes from Alice Bailey's *Esoteric Healing*, pages 24-88. This work was originally published in 1953, and was reprinted by the Lucis Publishing Company, New York, in 1977.

death, the consciousness can withdraw into the emotional body and reside on the emotional plane.[3]

Knowledge of the subtle bodies is necessary in order to identify the cause of a physical illness. Several conditions in the etheric and emotional bodies that can lead to disease are listed in Table 2, such as congestion in the etheric body or criticism in the emotional body. Illness also can originate in the mental body, but this case is less frequent. However, there can be external causes for illness, including accidents, epidemics, malnutrition, and heredity.

Mental Plane

A person has three focal points of perception on the fifth or mental plane. The first focal point of perception is *the mental body,* sometimes called the lower concrete mind, and it is built of particles from the lowest four divisions of the mental plane. The mental body deals with knowledge, particulars, or what are called concrete thoughts: for instance, a particular tree, car, or triangle. In contrast, the causal body (see below) is concerned with principles or abstract thoughts: trees or cars in general, or the principle of triangularity common to all triangles. The mental body has the following functions: to serve as the vehicle for concrete thinking; to express concrete thoughts through the emotional body, etheric brain, and dense physical brain; to develop the faculties of memory and imagination; and to function, as evolution proceeds, as a separate vehicle of consciousness on the mental plane.[4] Figure 1 defines the personality as consisting of the physical body (both dense and etheric), emotional body, and mental body, in which the mental body is the highest aspect of the personality.

The causal body, sometimes called the egoic lotus or soul, is the storehouse for the abstracted essence, or wisdom, gained from a person's experiences, and so it gradually evolves over time. It is referred to in the Bible as the "house not made with hands, eternal in the heavens" (2 Cor. 5:1). Only matter of the third subplane is vivified in the causal body of an undeveloped person, as indicated in Figure 1, but matter from the second subplane is brought into activity as evolution proceeds, so that the causal body can eventually extend over the second and third mental subplanes. Because the causal body is the vehicle for abstract thinking, an unevolved person is capable of only a limited amount of such thinking; whereas a great philosopher, who has higher matter active in his causal body, is capable of profound thought involving loftiness, subtlety, and wisdom. Another function of the causal body is sending to the upper brain the consciousness stream, which enables a person to be aware of himself, his thoughts, and his feelings. And when the causal body is sufficiently evolved, it can transmit qualities from higher planes to the personality.[5]

The spiritual mind, sometimes called the higher abstract mind, consists of matter from only the highest mental subplane. The spiritual mind reflects the innate divine nature with clarity, synthesis, and inclusiveness. When this mind is evoked, the person is able to perceive all forms in their correct perspective, and to apprehend reality with a clarity that is undistorted by illusions and glamours. The spiritual mind has two functions: to have intuitive insights, which are clear and direct perceptions of truths; and to convey clarity to abstract thinking by the causal body and to concrete thinking by the mental body.[6]

To summarize, the mental body is concerned with *knowledge* or concrete thinking; the causal body is concerned with *wisdom,* which is the abstracted result of long experience; and the spiritual mind is concerned with *insights,* which are the clear and direct perceptions of truths.

Higher Planes

According to theosophy, the real self is the monad, which is sometimes called the spirit, and it is a unit of consciousness, a spark of the Supreme Fire. The world of the monad is the second or monadic plane, but the roots of its life are in the first or adi plane. It may seem that the monad is far away; and yet according to this theory it is a person's self, the innermost source of his being, the wellspring of his life.[7]

The expression "consciousness on a plane" means the power of responding to the vibrations of that particular plane. It must be remembered that all seven planes interpenetrate. A person who is conscious on the physical plane often is totally unconscious on higher planes because he has not sufficiently organized his higher bodies to receive and transmit higher vibrations. Similarly, a monad, prior to its evolutionary cycle, is conscious on the second plane but is totally unconscious on the five lower planes.[8]

In order to develop its consciousness on the lower five planes, a monad may choose to initiate its evolutionary cycle, which begins as unconscious involution into these lower planes, followed by conscious evolution out of these planes. Because a monad has free choice, it is self-moved and self-directed in its entry into the lower planes of matter, which is the field of manifestation or the fivefold universe.[9]

As illustrated in Figure 1, a monad possesses three qualities of consciousness: will, love-wisdom, and active intelligence. At the beginning of the evolutionary cycle, these qualities create vibratory waves that cause matter to vibrate on the third, fourth, and fifth planes. The matter that vibrates on the third, or atmic, plane is called the "atmic permanent atom" and represents the spiritual will; the matter that vibrates on the fourth or buddhic plane is called the "buddhic permanent atom" and represents spiritual love; and the matter that vibrates on the fifth or mental plane is called the "mental permanent atom" and represents the spiritual mind.[10]

Spiritual will, spiritual love, and spiritual mind taken together form what is called the "spiritual triad," which is also sometimes called the individuality or transpersonality:

The **spiritual will** expresses the will quality from the monad, and it should be contrasted with desire, which expresses the self-centered motivation for the personality. When evoked, the spiritual will becomes an immanent, propulsive, clarifying, and driving force concerned with establishing right human relations and destroying whatever is hindering the free flow of life.[11]

The **spiritual love** expresses the love-wisdom quality from the monad, and it is neither sentiment nor affection. When evoked, the spiritual love eliminates the sense of separateness, allows the divine germ to be seen in all forms, enables the fact of group inclusiveness (or the essential unity of all beings) to be perceived, and results in true compassion.[12]

The **spiritual mind** expresses the active intelligence quality from the monad, and it was described in the previous section. When evoked, the spiritual mind conveys clarity to abstract thinking by the causal body and concrete thinking by the mental body.

The word *reflection* is used when a force manifested on a higher plane is passed down to a lower level, where it is conditioned by a grosser kind of matter, so that some of the effective power is lost in the reflected force. The spiritual triad reflects the nature of the monad and is the channel through which the monad functions in the field of manifestation. The spiritual triad could be viewed as a germ of divine life, containing the potentialities that later will be unfolded into powers during the course of evolution. At the beginning of the evolutionary cycle, the spiritual triad has the latency of a newly planted seed; but at the end, this seed will become a beautiful flower fully expressing its form, color, and perfume. There are several stages to this evolutionary cycle, which might be designated as pre-human, human, and post-human. [13]

Figure 1 illustrates the relationships that exist during the human stage of evolution. This diagram indicates that the spiritual triad (spiritual will, spiritual love, and spiritual mind) embraces the atmic plane, buddhic plane, and highest mental subplane. On the other hand, the personality (mental body, emotional body, etheric body, and dense physical body) embraces the four lowest mental subplanes, emotional plane, and physical plane. Thus, there exists a gap, extending over two mental subplanes, between the spiritual triad and personality. Two different "bridges" spanning this gap have been described:

The sutratma is the direct stream of life flowing from the monad, through the spiritual triad and causal body, to the personality, where it finds its anchor in the etheric heart. This life stream controls the circulation of blood throughout the physical body. [14] The sutratma is defined in Sanskrit as "the thread that binds all the selves in the human being with the divine," and it is referred to in the Bible as the "silver cord" (Eccles. 12:6).

The causal body, in an evolved condition, enables the personality to evoke the spiritual will, spiritual love, and spiritual mind. The causal body can be thought of as being an "illumined bridge" that is built through meditation, service, and constant efforts to draw forth insights.[15]

To summarize, man is in essence the *monad* (or spirit), reflecting as the *spiritual triad* in the field of manifestation, demonstrating through the gradually evolving *causal body* (or soul), and utilizing the *personality* as a means to contact the lower three planes for gaining experience. Thus, the person on the physical plane is the monad but expresses himself with his spiritual triad, causal body, and personality. Because the monad has free choice, the person on the physical plane also has free choice, which is his spiritual heritage. The person evolves by making decisions and learning from the effects (either good or bad) of those decisions.

As mentioned earlier, the purpose of evolution is to develop consciousness. In the case of the human stage of evolution, the purpose is to evolve the causal body, which means to gain wisdom from experiences. Whereas the monad, spiritual triad, and causal body are all free from internal conflict, it is obvious that the personality is often full of wickedness, disease, and despair; but this situation occurs only because of a gap, or lack of evolution, in the causal body.[16] In other words, the potential nature of a person is divinity; but because of ignorance about his true nature, he may create for himself many difficulties. The purpose of evolution is to face these problems and to grow in wisdom by overcoming them. Thus, according to this perspective, all problems eventually have a beneficent effect and play a positive role. As the Bible puts it, a man is made "perfect through sufferings" (Heb. 2:10).

Although this discussion concerning evolution of monads may seem abstruse, the process of unconscious involution followed by conscious evolution occurs every day, with any addiction, indulgence, or negative emotion. A man begins an addiction to gain experience, completely ignorant about the harm he is doing to himself; after he hits "rock bottom," his suffering forces him consciously to undo and retrace all of his previous steps; eventually he emerges free from his addiction, as he was prior to his descent, and his entire experience results in new wisdom. And so it is said that the monad is ignorant concerning the five lower planes of manifestation and chooses to in-volve into these lower planes, that the resulting suffering from limitation eventually leads to evolution out of these lower planes, and that the entire cycle produces an expansion of consciousness. This same theme is described in the Bible as the parable of the prodigal son (Luke 15:11-32).

What implications does this philosophy have for healing?

Disease has a positive contribution or lesson to give to the patient. A person is able to grow in wisdom only by learning from his problems. Each problem is actually an ingredient for a future attainment. Consequently, there need be no antagonism toward a disease.

Disease has no real existence or power. It only seems to exist because of the patient's ignorance concerning his own spiritual nature. But if the gap in the causal body were filled, then the apparent disease would soon disappear. Thus, true healing lies in an illumination of the patient rather than in a battle with disease. However, the patient may not be in a condition or at a point of evolution where such illumination is possible. In such a case it may be appropriate to apply palliatives and ameliorating methods that aid in building up the form life and fostering vitality. These methods can include allopathic or homeopathic remedies or the pranic healing approach described in Chapter 4, but all of these may give only temporary results. On the other hand, the telepathic and radiatory approaches described in Chapters 5 and 6 may assist in the patient's illumination, thereby bringing about lasting results. Thus, it may be appropriate for a healer to work on several levels at the same time.

All healing is self-healing; in the last analysis the patient must heal himself. Indeed, the very purpose of evolution is for each person to grow in consciousness by overcoming his limitations. Nevertheless, a healer can still play a useful role as a catalyst who assists the patient in achieving his goal. In chemistry a catalyst is defined as a substance that remains unchanged while increasing the rate of reaction between other substances. For instance, enzymes act as catalysts in the digestion of food, enabling chemical changes to take place in their presence. Although the patient must heal himself, the healing process may be facilitated by the catalytic presence of an esoteric healer.

Chapter 2

Etheric Chakras

This chapter will consider the etheric chakras, including their functions, locations, and relationships with endocrine glands. This information will emphasize the form aspect of physical life but will provide the background needed for all later topics. In contrast, the next chapter will consider the consciousness aspect.

Functions

Bailey describes the etheric body as follows: "The etheric body is a body composed entirely of lines of force and of points where these lines of force cross each other and thus form (in crossing) centres of energy."[1]

In Sanskrit these lines of force are called *nadis,* and the centers of energy are called *chakras.* The nadis constitute an extensive intangible network of energies, and it is said that the physical nervous system is an externalization of the nadis. Where only a few lines of force intersect, then only a minor chakra is formed. But where great streams of energy meet and cross, as they do in the head and along the spine, then a major chakra is formed.

The seven major chakras are listed in Table 3 on page 14 along with their associated locations, forces, and dense organs. These centers

Table 3. Major Etheric Chakras*

Chakra	Approximate Location	Type of Force	Dense Organs
Crown	Top of head	Spiritual will Synthetic Dynamic	Upper brain Right eye
Brow	Between eyebrows, in front of head	Soul force Vision Magnetic Light Intuition	Lower brain Left eye Nose Nervous system
Throat	Back of neck	Creative energy Sound	Breathing apparatus Alimentary canal
Heart	Between shoulder blades	Life force Group consciousness	Heart Circulatory system Blood Vagus nerve
Solar Plexus	Well below shoulder blades	Astral force Emotion Desire Touch	Stomach Liver Gallbladder Nervous system
Sacral	Lower part of lumbar area	Life force Physical plane force Vital energy Animal life	Sex organs
Basic	Base of spine	Will energy Universal life Kundalini	Kidneys Spinal column

*The material in this table was adapted from Alice Bailey's *Esoteric Healing*, page 45, published by the Lucis Publishing Company, New York, in 1977.

are crown, brow, throat, heart, solar plexus, sacral, and basic. However, different names are sometimes used by other authors.

The twenty-one minor chakras are listed in Table 4 on page 16 along with their associated locations. However, only four of these will be referred to in subsequent chapters: the two centers that together constitute the splenic chakra and the two centers in the palms of the hands. In fact, many authors count the splenic chakra, instead of the sacral, as being one of the seven major centers.

The emotional and mental bodies also have force centers that are counterparts of the centers in the etheric body. But unless explicitly stated otherwise, the word *chakra* throughout this book will refer only to an etheric force center and not to a center on a higher plane.

Each of the seven major chakras vitalizes its nearby area of the physical body, both etheric and dense portions, including minor chakras and dense organs. Table 3 lists some of the dense organs associated with each chakra. The health of an organ is viewed as dependent on the condition of its associated chakra, for example, whether the chakra is balanced, overstimulated, or understimulated.

A major chakra evolves over time and moves from a sluggish semidormant state to an active fully developed state. When a chakra develops, it gains the ability to work with additional forces and to perform additional functions. Some forces associated with each major chakra are listed in Table 3. Following are summaries of some of the functions of each of the seven major chakras, plus the splenic chakra, in both undeveloped and developed states:

The crown chakra vitalizes the cerebrum (or upper brain) and anchors the consciousness stream from the causal body. When developed, it registers wisdom from the causal body, insights from the spiritual mind, and dedication for selfless service from the spiritual will.

The brow chakra vitalizes the cerebellum (or lower brain) and central nervous system (which consists of nerve fibers within the brain stem and spinal cord). When developed, this chakra focuses wisdom, insights, and dedication for selfless service (all received via the crown chakra), which then can be used to control and dominate the personality. The brow is not the organ of creation in the same sense that the throat center is, but instead it expresses the intention to create that lies behind active creativity.

Table 4. Minor Etheric Chakras*

Minor Chakras	Location on the Physical Body
2	"There are two in front of the ears, close to where the jaw bones are connected."
2	"There are two just above the two breasts."
1	"There is one where the breast bone connects, close to the thyroid gland. This, with the two breast centres, makes a triangle of force."
2	"There are two, one each in the palms of the hands."
2	"There are two, one each in the soles of the feet."
2	"There are two, just behind the eyes."
2	"There are two, also, connected with the gonads."
1	"There is one close to the liver."
1	"There is one connected with the stomach; it is related, therefore, to the solar plexus, but is not identical with it."
2	"There are two connected with the spleen. These form one centre in reality, but such a centre is formed by the two being superimposed one on the other."
2	"There are two—one at the back of each knee."
1	"There is one powerful centre which is closely connected with the vagus nerve. This is most potent and is regarded by some schools of occultism as a major centre; it is not in the spine, but is no great distance from the thymus gland."
1	"There is one which is close to the solar plexus, and relates it to the centre at the base of the spine, thus making a triangle of the sacral centre, the solar plexus, and the centre at the base of the spine."

*The material in this table was adapted from Alice Bailey's *Esoteric Healing*, pages 465-466, published by the Lucis Publishing Company, New York, in 1977.

The throat chakra vitalizes the lungs and vocal apparatus, and it also registers concrete thoughts from the mental body (received via the solar plexus chakra). When developed, the throat chakra responds to strength and clarity from the causal body (received via the brow chakra), enabling creativity to be expressed in thought, speech, and writing.

The heart chakra anchors the life stream (sutratma) from the monad, and this stream controls the circulation of blood, which in turn feeds the individual cells of the body. This chakra both vitalizes and controls the vagus nerve, the largest nerve in the parasympathetic nervous system (which activates involuntary muscles that restore the body's energy). When developed, it registers compassion from the spiritual love, which is experienced as a sense of oneness with others.

The solar plexus chakra vitalizes the sympathetic nervous system (which activates involuntary muscles that mobilize the body for action). This chakra is considered to be developed in an average or ordinary human being, in which case it registers emotions that can incorporate both feelings from the emotional body and concrete thoughts from the mental body.

The splenic chakra assimilates prana (which will be discussed in Chapter 4) from the atmosphere, which then vitalizes the entire system of major and minor chakras. It is considered to be in a developed state for all human beings.

The sacral chakra vitalizes the sexual life and organs of reproduction. It also is considered to be developed.

The basic chakra vitalizes the kidneys. This chakra also feeds the life-giving principle, the will to live, to all parts of the physical body, resulting in the fundamental instinct of self-preservation. When developed, it allows the dedication for selfless service from the spiritual will to be registered continually by the crown chakra.[2]

As indicated by the foregoing list, only the crown, heart, and solar plexus chakras can directly receive energies from higher planes. Any other chakra can receive a higher plane energy only after the energy has initially been registered by one of these three chakras.[3]

Because each major chakra can vitalize or control a portion of the dense physical body, it might be expected that a person who has developed a particular chakra would display some abnormality in the activity of his associated organs, in the sense that this activity would somehow be different from that of a person with an undeveloped chakra. Although contemporary science is unable to detect the presence of a chakra directly, it may be possible with contemporary instruments to detect differences in the activity of organs associated with a chakra. In this way it may be possible to draw inferences as to the physiological effects of chakra development and whether a particular chakra is or is not developed.

Motoyama has reported this type of experimental research.[4] He showed that there were several physiological differences among a group of individuals said to have developed their heart chakra when compared with another group not having this development.

Locations

Several authors have described the locations of the chakras. Leadbeater states that the etheric body projects slightly beyond the outline of the dense physical body and that the major centers appear as rotating "wheels," "saucer-like depressions," or "vortices" in its surface. This description justifies the name *chakra*, as it means wheel in Sanskrit. He also says that a major chakra has a diameter of about two inches when undeveloped and a larger size after development.[5]

Bailey also indicates that the etheric body extends outside the dense physical body and that the chakras are part of that portion of the etheric body that lies outside. In particular, she states that the crown chakra is "just above the top of the head"; the brow chakra is "just in front of the eyes and forehead"; and the five spinal chakras (throat, heart, solar plexus, sacral, and basic) are positioned in the "etheric counterpart of the spinal column," which is behind the dense physical body.[6] In addition, she says that these spinal centers are at least two inches away from the dense physical spine for an undeveloped person and are even further away for an average person.[7]

Unfortunately, Bailey never published a diagram showing the locations of the chakras according to her perspective. However, Tansley does illustrate the locations of the major chakras in Figure 2. His diagram is consistent with Bailey's written description in the following

Crown

Ajna

Throat

Heart

Solar plexus

Sacral

Base

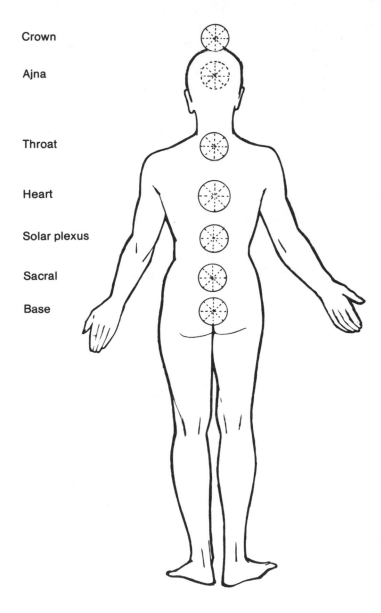

Figure 2. Locations of Major Etheric Chakras. (Adapted from D.V. Tansley's *Radionics and the Subtle Anatomy of Man,* page 29. This work was first published in 1972, and was reprinted in 1980 by the Health Science Press, Essex, England.)

way: the five spinal centers are represented with solid lines, which indicate that these centers are behind the body; and the brow (or ajna) center is represented with a broken line, which indicates that it is in front of the body.[8]

On the other hand, some authors have claimed that the chakras are in positions quite different from those indicated by Bailey's description and Tansley's diagram. In fact, Bailey herself acknowledges that the "average psychic" regards the solar plexus and throat chakras as being in front of the body.[9] For the purposes of the present study, the chakras will be considered as being in the locations indicated by Bailey and Tansley, with the spinal chakras being about three inches behind the dense physical spine for an average person.

Endocrine Glands

The physical body has four main systems for distributing energy:

The etheric vehicle, with its lines of force and its seven major chakras as focal points for energy registration and distribution

The nervous system, including the central, sympathetic, and parasympathetic branches

The endocrine gland system, which serves to regulate various aspects of the body through the secretion of hormones

The blood system, which carries the energies from the three foregoing systems throughout the dense physical body[10]

This section will examine the relationship between the endocrine glands and the chakras. A gland is defined as endocrine if it forms a specific substance and secretes this substance into the blood and if this substance exerts a specific effect on some organ or process at a distance from the gland. This specific substance is called a hormone, and it can be viewed as being a chemical messenger from the gland to the target organ or process.

The nonendocrine glands of the body have well-defined ducts (or channels) that act as passageways from each gland to a single point. For

Table 5. Associations between Etheric Chakras and Endocrine Glands, According to Various Sources*

Chakra	Associated Endocrine Gland				
	Bailey	Beasley	Chaney	Gardner	Schwarz
Crown	Pineal	Pineal	Pineal	Pineal	Pineal
Brow	Pituitary	Pituitary	Pituitary	Pituitary	Pituitary
Throat	Thyroid	Thyroid, parathyroid	Thyroid	Thyroid	Thyroid
Heart	Thymus	Thymus	Thymus	Thymus	Thymus
Solar plexus	Pancreas	Adrenals, pancreas	Liver	Adrenals	Adrenals
Splenic	Spleen	Spleen	Spleen	Spleen, pancreas	Spleen
Sacral	Gonads	Gonads	—	—	Gonads
Basic	Adrenals	—	Adrenals, gonads	Gonads, pituitary	—

*The sources used for this table are as follows: the Bailey material comes from *Esoteric Healing*, page 142; Beasley's material from *Subtle-Body Healing*, page 36; E. C. Chaney's associations are from "Treasures on the Tree of Life" (*Astara's Book of Life*, volume 2, number 9), pages 1-7; the Gardner material is from *Vital Magnetic Healing*, page 7; and Schwarz' associations are from *Human Energy Systems*, page 14. For full publication data, the reader is referred to the Bibliography.

Table 6. Functions of Endocrine Glands*

Gland	Hormone	Function or Effect
Anterior pituitary	Thyrotropic (TSH)	Stimulates the thyroid gland to secrete its hormones.
	Adrenocorticotropic (ACTH)	Stimulates the adrenal center to produce its hormones.
	Melanocyte-stimulating hormone (MSH)	Function in man is uncertain.
	Follicle-stimulating hormone (FSH)	Stimulates the maturation of the ovum and production of estrogen in the female. Stimulates sperm development in the male.
	Luteinizing hormone (LH)	Triggers release of the mature ovum and production of progesterone and estrogen in the female. Stimulates testosterone secretion in the male.
	Lactogenic hormone (LTH)	Stimulates milk production in the female. Also acts like growth hormone.
	Growth hormone	Controls general body growth and affects fat, protein, and carbohydrate metabolism.
Posterior pituitary	Oxytocin	Stimulates the contraction of uterine muscles during birth and causes ejection of milk.
	Vasopressin	Primary control of water reabsorption from the kidney tubule and causes contraction of smooth muscles.
Hypothalamus	Neurohormones	Triggers the release of pituitary tropic hormones.
Adrenal cortex	Cortisone and cortisol	Help control glucose—glycogen balances, water balance, protein utilization, and general metabolism.
	Aldosterone	Controls mineral balance, mainly sodium and potassium.

Table 6, continued

Gland	Hormone	Function or Effect
Adrenal medulla	Epinephrine	Excites the nervous system, circulatory system, and increases release of glucose from the liver.
	Norepinephrine	Increases metabolic rate, constricts blood vessels.
Thyroid	Thyroxine	Controls carbohydrate metabolism.
Parathyroid	Parathormone	Regulates calcium and potassium metabolism.
Pancreas	Insulin	Increases glycogen storage in the liver, decreases blood sugar, affects water balance, primary factor in regulating glucose passages into cells.
	Glucagon	Stimulates release of glucose from the liver.
Ovary	Estrogen	Initiate preparation of the uterus for fertilized egg, stimulate and maintain female secondary sex characteristics.
	Progesterone	Necessary to prevent abortion of the embryo and stimulate final preparation of the uterus for the fertilized egg.
Placenta	Chorionic gonadotropin	Acts with other female sex hormones to maintain pregnancy.
Ovary and placenta	Relaxin	Relaxes the ligaments of the pelvis to enlarge the birth canal passage.
Testes	Androgen	Stimulates and maintains male secondary sex characteristics.
Digestive tract	Secretin	Stimulates the release of pancreatic juice.

*The material in this table is adapted from *Hormones*, by R. LeBaron, pages 152-156. This work was published by Bobbs-Merrill, New York, in 1972.

example, the salivary glands pour saliva into the mouth through tubelike ducts. In contrast, the endocrine glands are ductless and must use the blood vessels of the body as their communication channels. The cells of endocrine glands are in close contact with blood capillaries and pour their hormones directly into these vessels. Thus, endocrine hormones have a much wider distribution than do nonendocrine products.

Both the endocrine system and nervous system help to coordinate the functioning of organs and processes in separate parts of the dense physical body. However, there is an important qualitative difference in the activity of these two systems. The endocrine system builds up by secretion an effective blood concentration of its active chemicals, the hormones, and this concentration is maintained for appreciable lengths of time. Thus, the endocrine system is involved in slow-starting, long-lasting responses. On the other hand, the nervous system uses chains of neurons as its medium of communication, and this arrangement allows high-speed, short-duration responses.

What is the relationship between the endocrine glands and the chakras? Chaney considers these glands to be the dense physical counterparts of the chakras: "The etheric chakras are the glands of the etheric body. The glands of the physical form are the crystalized counterparts and instruments for the chakras."[11] Gardner views the glands as being influenced by the chakras: "In practice it has been observed that the condition of a chakram, viewed clairvoyantly or diagnosed by touch, has a definite influence upon the endocrine glands lying within its sphere of influence."[12] And Bailey makes the connection between the glands and the art of healing:

> One of the effects of the application of the healing energy (through the medium of any centre conditioning the area wherein the point of friction is located) is the stimulation of the related gland and its increased activity. The glands are intermediaries, in the last analysis, between the healer and the patient, between the centre and the dense physical body, and between the etheric body and its automaton, the receiving dense physical vehicle.[13]

In the above quotation, the term *centre* refers to one of the major etheric chakras.

In Table 5 on page 21, several writers associate a specific endocrine gland with each of the major chakras. No two of these writers agree completely, and this situation indicates at least that these sources are independent. One explanation for some of these differences is that Bailey considers the splenic to be a minor chakra, whereas the other writers consider it to be one of the seven major chakras.

The following observation can be made from Table 5: writers on chakras frequently contradict each other. Thus, the reader is advised to be skeptical regarding the validity of all sources of chakra information. However, it is the viewpoint here that Bailey's information in this table is correct.

Table 6 on pages 22-23 lists the known hormones and functions, according to a current book in endocrinology, for some of the glands included in Table 5. When examining Table 6, it is helpful to note the following: The pituitary gland has two lobes, anterior and posterior, and the hormones are listed separately for each lobe. Because the pituitary secretes nine known hormones, with some affecting other glands, the pituitary is often called the "master gland" of the body. The adrenal gland also has two parts: the outer part, called the cortex, surrounds the central portion (medulla), and the hormones are listed separately for each of these parts. The gonads refer to the testes in males and ovaries in females, which is how they are listed in Table 6.

The pineal, thymus, liver, and spleen are included in Table 5 but not in Table 6. Current endocrinology considers the pineal and thymus as being probable endocrine glands, but the precise functions of their hormones are not well understood. Perhaps this ignorance results from the fact that these glands do not function fully in an adult until their corresponding chakras are developed.[14] Although the liver and spleen are known to add important materials to the blood, they are not currently viewed as being endocrine glands.

Chapter 3

States of Consciousness

This chapter will examine the relationships between the etheric chakras and the consciousness aspect of physical life, including such topics as evolution of conciousness, effects of meditation and self-hypnosis, and differences between spiritual development and psychic opening.

Evolution of Consciousness

A way of understanding human consciousness is to contrast it with animal experience. It has been noted that free choice and "moments of reflection" are present in human consciousness but that these are absent in animals because their behavior and memory are both instinctive.[1] Another name for the moment of reflection is self-awareness, and the latter term will be used in this chapter. Self-awareness is a type of awareness that is independent of mental activity and enables us to be aware of ourselves, our thoughts, and our feelings.

The spiritual will is another quality that can be present in human consciousness while absent in animals. The spiritual will reflects the intrinsic wholeness and oneness of life; and it is a conscious inner impulse for establishing harmony and right relationships. In contrast, animals have an unconscious sense of unity with nature.[2]

This section will consider the evolution of human consciousness. Ouspensky defines the following four states: sleep, relative consciousness, self-consciousness, and objective consciousness. He points out that sleep and relative consciousness are generally the only two states in which a man lives, and that the states of self-consciousness and objective consciousness become accessible only after a hard and prolonged struggle.[3]

These four states of consciousness can be interpreted from the standpoint of cognition. While in the first state of sleep, which is purely subjective and passive, nothing can be known regarding the external world. In the second state, or relative consciousness, the person is awake but his understanding is distorted, so that he can know only relative truth. In the third state, or self-consciousness, he can know the full truth about himself. And in the fourth state, or objective consciousness, he can know the full truth about the world.[4]

These four states also can be interpreted from the standpoint of the two qualities described earlier: self-awareness and spiritual will. In the sleep state, a man has neither self-awareness nor spiritual will. In the second or relative state, he has glimpses of both self-awareness and spiritual will, which are followed by long intervals of what could be called inattention. In the third state (self-consciousness), he continually experiences self-awareness but has only glimpses of spiritual will. And in the fourth state (objective consciousness), he continually experiences both self-awareness and spiritual will.

Even though the average awake person is only in the relative consciousness state, he may think of himself as being in the self-consciousness state. In fact, if a person were asked whether or not he is conscious of himself, he probably will answer that he is conscious and be correct. He will be correct because the question has made him vaguely self-aware for that moment, but the next moment his self-awareness will disappear, although he may still remember his answer and think of himself as being self-aware. The difficulty is that when a person is inattentive he is unable to know that he is inattentive; instead it takes a glimpse of self-awareness to enable a person to realize that he previously was inattentive.[5] As an analogy, a person who is dreaming is generally unaware that he is dreaming; instead he must awaken before he can realize that he previously was dreaming.

Consequently, the first obstacle that a person faces in attaining self-consciousness is his conviction that he already possesses that state. The following experiment is suggested for proving that a person is generally not aware of himself. The experimenter should take a watch and follow the movement of the second hand while at the same time remaining self-aware. This experiment is not the same as the practice of concentration, where effort is made only to focus on some object; such concentration can be maintained for a considerable length of time, especially if it becomes hypnotic absorption. Rather, in this experiment, the person tries to maintain awareness simultaneously of both the watch and himself. Ouspensky says that an average person can do this experiment for only about two minutes, which is the limit of his self-awareness. Furthermore, if he tries to repeat this experiment soon afterward, he will find it more difficult than the first time.[6] This experiment demonstrates that the average person has only relative consciousness, which means that he can experience only brief glimpses of self-awareness.

This chapter will employ Ouspensky's terminology except that the second state of relative consciousness will be divided into six distinct states, so that there will be nine states altogether. Table 7 on page 30 lists all nine states of consciousness and relates them to developed chakras, kingdoms of nature, and initiations.

Each of the last seven states listed in Table 7 is expressed via the development of a major chakra. After each chakra develops, the person is able to register an additional quality from a dimension higher than the physical, enabling him to experience an expansion of consciousness.

Seven kingdoms of nature have been described, each kingdom having its own unique set of characteristics.[7] However, only four kingdoms are important in this section: vegetable, animal, human, and soul. Table 7 indicates that a person can experience a state of awareness corresponding to each of these four kingdoms of nature.

The word *initiation* refers to an expansion of awareness that results from the person's own effort, rather than being something conferred on him by another. Although nine spiritual initiations have been described, only the first five initiations can be experienced by a member of the human kingdom, and thus only these five are included in Table 7. Although there are Christian mystical, Buddhist, and Hindu names for

Table 7. States of Consciousness

State of Consciousness	Description	Kingdom of Nature	Developed Chakra	Initiation	Christian Mysticism	Buddhism	Hinduism
Sleep	Sentiency without awareness	Vegetable	—	—	—	—	—
Hypnosis	Awareness of the environment; neither self-awareness nor spiritual will	Animal	—	—	—	—	—
Sensual	Glimpses of self-awareness and spiritual will; identification with physical body and pursuit of sensual gratification	Human	Sacral	—	—	—	—
Aesthetic	Aesthetic appreciation; pursuit of pride and vanity	Human	Solar Plexus	—	—	—	—
Compassionate	Sense of compassion for others	Human	Heart	First	Birth at Bethlehem	Sotapatti	Parivrajaka
Creative	Clarity in thought and speech; creativity in some endeavor	Human	Throat	Second	Baptism in Jordan	Sakadagamin	Kitichaka
Intuitive	Ease in expressing intuitive wisdom	Human	Brow	Third	Transfiguration	Anagamin	Hamsa
Self-Consciousness	Constant state of self-awareness; awareness of full truth about oneself	Human	Crown	Fourth	Crucifixion	Arhat	Paramahamsa
Objective Consciousness	Constant state of spiritual will; awareness of full truth about objective world	Soul	Basic	Fifth	Resurrection	Asekha	Jivanmukhta

these initiations, only the Christian mystical terms are utilized in the discussion that follows.[8]

The nine states of consciousness are:

The sleep state: the lowest state listed in Table 7. Here, the physical body has both vitality and sentiency, but lacks awareness. In other words, the body has a sensitive response to contact, but does not have any cognitive perception of the environment. This condition is similar to that of the vegetable kingdom and of the beginning human embryo.

The hypnotic state: the second state listed in Table 7. Now the person has awareness of the environment, but lacks self-awareness and spiritual will. This condition is similar to that of the animal kingdom and of the human fetus prior to birth. While awaking from sleep or falling asleep, the hypnotic state is temporarily experienced. Hypnosis also can be deliberately induced in various ways (by autosuggestion, for example).

The sensual state: the first state to be experienced following birth. The sacral chakra becomes developed around the time of birth, enabling the person to have postnatal glimpses of self-awareness and spiritual will, which together are sometimes called "the voice of conscience." The presence of these two qualities is a distinguishing feature of the human kingdom as compared with the animal kingdom. In this state, the person is identified with his dense physical body and often pursues goals of sensual gratification, although his conscience enables him to discriminate between responsible and irresponsible behavior. By following the guidance of his conscience, he can attain higher states of consciousness, which progressively reveal more of his spiritual identity.[9]

The aesthetic state: this is the condition of the average person (except for infants and raw savages), and it corresponds to a developed solar plexus chakra. The person can appreciate artistic, cultural, and musical activities, but often indulges in such negative emotions as fear, guilt, and anger. He mainly pursues self-centered goals of pride and vanity, resulting in inner conflicts and competition with others. After experiencing the pain associated with self-centered living, the person may seek a higher way. Thus, he may endeavor to be detached and objective toward his physical behavior, acknowledge his competitiveness as well as his feelings engendering that behavior, and then try expressing cooperative feelings.[10]

The compassionate state: this is associated with a developed heart chakra and the first spiritual initiation called "Birth at Bethlehem." The person is able to experience spiritual love, which is compassion or a sense of oneness with others. As a result, he is able to discipline his physical behavior, so that he generally acts in a moral and ethical way. But because of remaining self-centered goals, he often regresses into lower states of consciousness. The person has attained only the "birth" of a spiritual way of living, but not its full maturity, producing inner conflicts between his new realization and his lower nature. Consequently, the person may seek a higher level of self-mastery by resolving his emotional conflicts in the following way: becoming detached and objective toward his feelings; identifying the concrete thoughts and beliefs that underlie or are responsible for his conflicted feelings; and then using his mental body to change those thoughts and beliefs, leading to different feelings.[11]

The creative state: corresponds to a developed throat chakra and the second initiation called "Baptism in Jordan." The person's causal body conveys strength and clarity to his mental body, enabling concrete thinking to be expressed in a creative way. The word "baptism" signifies purification. The person can now more easily purify his emotional nature and function as an integrated personality. However, he may sense a new limitation: concrete thinking can be distorted by illusions and self-deceptions. Thus, he may seek a higher level of self-mastery by becoming detached and objective towards his concrete thoughts, and then using the wisdom of his causal body to appraise and guide the concrete thinking of his mental body.[12]

The intuitive state: corresponds to a developed brow chakra and the third initiation called "Transfiguration." The person's spiritual mind conveys clarity to abstract thinking by his causal body, enabling intuitive wisdom to be expressed easily. Consequently, he can function as an integrated causal body and personality, which is a new or "transfigured" state of being. However, he may sense a new limitation: the expression of wisdom can be inadequate, because it is a response of memory rather than a direct perception of truth. As a result, the person may seek a further level of self-mastery by becoming detached and objective toward his abstract thoughts, and then using the insights of his spiritual mind to appraise and guide the wisdom of his causal body.[13]

The self-consciousness state: corresponds to a developed crown chakra and the fourth initiation called "Crucifixion." The person has continuous self-awareness, which means continuous detached awareness of his abstract thoughts, concrete thoughts, emotional feelings, and physical behavior. In earlier states, the person did not have this self-awareness in its present fullness because he was too strongly identified with either his causal body or personality. But in this state, he is no longer so identified. Consequently, he receives insights from his spiritual mind, which reveal the full truth about himself, leading to the death or "crucifixion" of his remaining false ideas, illusions, and self-deceptions. Through this process of self-awareness, the person may come to realize that the "self"—which he defends and cherishes, which can attack and be attacked—is only a concept that he made up. As a result, he may seek an even higher level of self-mastery by progressively relinquishing all self-centered goals from his life, without any sense of loss or regret. [14]

The objective consciousness state: associated with a developed basic chakra and the fifth initiation called "Resurrection." The person has relinquished all self-centeredness and instead expresses his spiritual will, which is experienced as an inner dedication toward performing impersonal service and establishing right human relationships. The spiritual will was available in earlier states of consciousness, but only in this final one does the person continually express this spiritual impulse. Consequently, he also continually expresses his spiritual love, and the full truth regarding the objective world is revealed by insights from his spiritual mind. Because the spiritual triad consists of the spiritual will, spiritual love, and spiritual mind, the person is now able to function as an integrated spiritual triad, causal body, and personality. He is now "resurrected" into a new kingdom of nature, the kingdom of souls, although he may still be functioning in a human body on the physical plane. [15]

Each of the foregoing states of consciousness has an associated quality. The quality for a lower state is less subtle than that for a higher state, but a lower state also includes glimpses of higher qualities. Each of the human states (namely, sensual through self-consciousness) has a sense of limitation that may motivate the person to attain his next higher state. And each state must unfold according to the order presented.

One implication of the chakra theory is that the possible human states of consciousness are finite and discrete. A chakra is either developed or undeveloped, and a person is able to reside in one or another state depending on how many of his chakras are developed. A precise definition of chakra development will be given in the following section.

Chakra Development

A person's causal body is the storehouse for the wisdom gained from all of his experiences. Thus, the condition of his causal body represents in a latent way his state of consciousness. But in order for a person to function on the physical plane, the condition of his causal body must be translated into energy movements within his etheric body. The preceding section described some of the specific realizations, or contents of the causal body, that represent the latent aspect of each human state of consciousness; this section will describe the energy flows in the etheric body that enable each state of awareness to be manifested physically.

Bailey states that each major chakra is separated from the one above it and the one below it by an interlaced protective web of etheric substance. She says that there are four circular webs lying between the five major chakras in the etheric spine and that there are two additional webs in the head. The substance of the webs in the head has a quality higher than that of the webs in the spine. When intact, these six webs prevent the free movement of energies in the etheric body.[16]

Kundalini is a Sanskrit word meaning "the sleeping divine power at the base of the spine," and this word denotes an important etheric energy produced by the basic chakra. The kundalini energy has three different phases: "coiled," when not stimulating any of the higher centers; "serpent of wisdom," when stimulating one or more of the higher centers, prior to the activation of the basic chakra; and "dragon of living fire," following the activation of the basic chakra. The four spinal webs impede the movement of the kundalini energy up the etheric spine.[17]

Bailey states that the etheric webs "are normally dissipated as purity of life, the discipline of the emotions and the development of the spiritual will are carried forward."[18] The sequence in which the etheric webs are dissipated determines the sequence in which the seven major chakras develop. Because the etheric webs do not affect the functioning of the minor chakras, all minor chakras, including the splenic, are always considered to be developed following birth. These minor chakras unfold during the fetal stage prior to birth.

Each state of consciousness is characterized by the continuous etheric registration of a particular energy from a plane higher than the physical. This continuous registration, performed by a major etheric chakra, gives an additional quality to the person's experience, although glimpses of this quality might be available in earlier states of consciousness. The word *registration* is used instead of *reception* to convey the fact that the etheric chakra must play an active role in "stepping down" the higher-plane energy. One effect of dissipating an etheric web is to enable an appropriate physical plane energy (such as kundalini) to reach a major chakra and thereby improve its registration of the higher-plane energy. The chakra converts the registered energy into a vibratory wave of one of the four ethers, which is the appropriate form for the etheric system.[19] As an analogy, a telephone receiver converts electrical impulses into sound waves, which is the appropriate form for an auditory system.

The lowest etheric web is between the basic and sacral chakras. When this web is dissipated, the sacral chakra is said to be developed. Because this dissipation occurs around the time of birth, the sacral chakra is always developed for all persons following birth. This dissipation of the web implies that a small amount of kundalini from the basic chakra can reach the sacral chakra so that the sacral can produce another energy, which Chaney calls the "Golden Oil" or the "Chrism."[20] This new energy can be transmitted to the crown chakra, thereby enabling the latter to register glimpses of self-awareness and spiritual will, which in turn constitute the conscience. Thus, the person is able to express the lowest human state of consciousness listed in Table 7, which is the sensual.

While the dissipation of the lowest etheric web occurs automatically at birth, the dissipation of each higher web generally takes place in the following way. Because each human state of consciousness has a sense of limitation that results in pain of some kind, the person may use his free choice to understand the cause of his suffering. If the person gains an additional insight regarding his condition, there results a new growth in his causal body, a new attitude toward life, a small change in the energy flows in his etheric body, and some wearing away of one of the remaining etheric webs. When sufficient growth in his causal body has been attained, the resulting etheric energy movements will cause sufficient pressure on a remaining web to pierce it. With the piercing of the web, the person will discover that a new quality can be registered continuously and without effort, which previously could be registered only briefly and with effort. Thus, he will be able to experience a higher state of awareness, which is the outer expression of inner growth that had earlier been achieved in his causal body.

The spinal webs can be dissipated by the progressive rising of the kundalini. For an average or ordinary human being, the etheric web between the sacral and solar plexus chakras has generally been dissipated, in which case the solar plexus chakra is said to be developed. Kundalini then can reach the solar plexus chakra, and the subsequent stimulation enables this center to register emotional sensitivity coming from the emotional body. When the web between the solar plexus and heart chakras is dissipated, the heart chakra is said to be developed. As a result, kundalini can reach and stimulate the heart chakra, enabling this center to register compassion from the spiritual love. When the web between the heart and throat chakras is dissipated, the throat chakra is said to be developed, and the kundalini can reach and stimulate the crown, brow, and throat chakras. The crown chakra then can register strength and clarity from the causal body, which can be passed down and focused by the brow chakra, enabling the mental body and throat chakra to express concrete thinking in a clear and creative way.[21]

In yoga philosophy, the etheric spinal column is said to consist of three channels having the following Sanskrit names: *pingala, ida,* and *sushumna*. Bailey identifies three different etheric energies that can flow through these spinal channels: the kundalini energy, sometimes called "the fire of matter" emanates from the basic chakra, has the ability to stimulate the major chakras and uses the pingala channel; "the fire of manas" emanates from the throat chakra, improves sensitivity to impressions and uses the ida channel; and "the fire of spirit" emanates from the crown chakra, embodies energies from the causal body, and uses the sushumna channel.[22]

The fire of manas is impeded by the etheric web lying between the throat and brow chakras. When this web is worn away, the brow chakra is considered to be developed, and the fire of manas can reach and stimulate both the crown and brow chakras. As a result, the crown chakra can easily register wisdom from the causal body, which in turn has received clarity from the spiritual mind. After being focused by the brow chakra, this wisdom can guide the person's thoughts, feelings, and actions.[23]

Bailey describes a triangle of three centers that can distribute and circulate energy in the head: the crown, brow, and alta major—the latter is a nerve center located in the medulla oblongata area at the base of the skull.[24] The final etheric web separates the brow chakra from the crown chakra. This web impedes the direct flow of the fire of spirit between the crown and brow chakras, although this energy can circulate indirectly via the alta major center. When this final web is worn away, the crown chakra is regarded as developed, and the three head centers can function as a single unity. As a result, the person can have continual self-awareness, as well as receive insights from his spiritual mind.[25]

The last etheric chakra to develop is the basic. Its productivity is affected by energies from other chakras and by the person's intention. After the other major chakras have developed, all inputs utilizable by the basic chakra are available in ample quantities. When, in addition, the person has eliminated all self-centered goals from his life, the basic chakra is considered to be developed. As a result, the kundalini energy is transformed into the "dragon of living fire," which surges up the spine to further stimulate each major chakra. The kundalini, described earlier as "the sleeping divine power," is now regarded as being "awake." The three fires of matter, manas, and spirit are now merged in the crown chakra, enabling this chakra to clearly register the dedication for selfless service from the spiritual will.[26]

The preceding discussion can be interpreted as follows: The fire of matter represents the personality, fire of manas represents the causal body, and fire of spirit represents the spiritual triad. The four lowest webs represent material lessons, and the two highest webs represent spiritual lessons. When all lessons have been mastered, so that the corresponding webs have been dissipated, the three fires can merge and the person can function as an integrated spiritual triad, causal body, and personality.

In summary, the major chakras develop in the following order: first sacral, then solar plexus, heart, throat, brow, crown, and finally basic. Except for the basic, each major chakra is defined here as being developed when its associated etheric web is dissipated. It does not follow, however, that dissipating these webs is desirable. The etheric webs have an important and beneficent function: they prevent a person's chakras from producing more energies than he has wisdom, purification, and physical condition to handle.

There are two ways that the etheric webs can be pierced. The first method is based on *evolving the causal body,* and the person does not focus any attention on the chakras or etheric webs. Instead he proceeds to gain wisdom from his experiences; purify his physical, emotional, and mental natures; practice meditation (which will be discussed in the next section); and follow the guidance of his spiritual will. As a consequence, his causal body will evolve, leading to new attitudes toward life, and the resulting shifting of energies in his etheric body will automatically cause the webs to be gradually worn away, one by one.

In the second method, the person has the *deliberate goal of tearing his etheric webs.* He may use special breathing and physical exercises, but mainly he attempts to tear these webs by deliberately willing the blocked energies to rise. Unfortunately, such an attempt may be successful. Bailey states that the resulting premature unfoldment may overstimulate the brain cells, and "such stimulation can produce insanity and the breaking down of the cellular structure of the brain, and through the over-activity of the cell life can also induce that internal friction between them which will eventuate in brain tumors and abscesses."[27] Thus, it is far better to follow the first method and allow the chakras to develop as the person's causal body evolves, rather than to tear prematurely the etheric webs. Nevertheless, there are systems of occultism that are based on deliberately tearing the webs, and the reader is advised to avoid those systems.

Meditation

Each time a person awakens from sleep, he recapitulates his entire evolutionary history by passing from sleep (corresponding to the stage of a beginning human embryo), through hypnosis (corresponding to the stage of an unborn fetus), through the lower states of human consciousness, until he finally regains the highest state that he has attained. As an act of free choice, a person can regress into any state of consciousness lower than his normal one; this regression is termed *self-hypnosis* when his consciousness has been lowered into the hypnotic state. Also as an act of free choice, a person can temporarily evoke a quality associated with a higher state of consciousness; this evocation is termed *meditation.* Thus, meditation, as defined here, is the direct opposite of self-hypnosis.

Having a regular daily period of meditation is a fruitful approach for developing the chakras and raising one's state of consciousness. Without meditation a person will still experience glimpses of qualities associated with higher states, but the purpose of meditation is to prolong and deepen those glimpses. A person who regularly practices meditation will increase the activity of an undeveloped chakra, although only a developed chakra can be sufficiently active to enable its associated quality to be expressed continually.

A person's meditation practice usually will evolve as his chakras develop, so that there will be a different approach for each state of consciousness that he attains. Table 8 on page 40 recommends a particular meditation practice for each of the nine states of consciousness. None of the listed meditations is passive in the sense that the meditator tries to do nothing; instead, the effort in each case is to evoke a quality associated with a higher state of consciousness.

Although Table 8 relates each recommended meditation to the highest chakra that a person has developed, none of the listed practices suggests using any chakra as a focal point of concentration. Prolonged concentration on a chakra may cause a change in activity of the associated endocrine gland, which in turn may cause the glandular and nervous systems to become unbalanced.[28] Thus it is much better to allow the chakras to develop naturally as the causal body evolves, rather than attempting to hasten the process by mentally concentrating on them.

The average person has attained the aesthetic state of consciousness, and thus the meditations listed in Table 8 for the first three states (sleep, hypnosis, and sensual) are part of his past history. Whenever a

Table 8. Recommended Meditations

State of Consciousness	Developed Chakra	Recommended Meditation
Sleep	—	Dreaming
Hypnosis	—	Instinctive effort to leave hypnotic state
Sensual	Sacral	Following the guidance of conscience
Aesthetic	Solar Plexus	Radiating positive regard as a service; and consideration of a seed thought
Compassionate	Heart	Consideration of a seed thought; and practicing self-awareness
Creative	Throat	Consideration of a seed thought; and practicing self-awareness
Intuitive	Brow	Practicing self-awareness; and selfless service
Self-Consciousness	Crown	Selfless service
Objective Consciousness	Basic	Intense selfless service

person awakens from sleep and regains his normal state of awareness, he must repeat in essence, albeit without effort, each meditation practice that resulted in a past attainment. But it is necessary to employ effort and discipline for those new practices that will result in higher states in the future.

Radiating positive regard is a meditation practice recommended by Table 8 for the aesthetic state of consciousness. The person can radiate emotional qualities via his solar plexus chakra, because this chakra is developed, and he may wish to proceed as follows: First, he selects a recipient, perhaps a leader in his community. Second, he relinquishes any personal reactions that he has to the recipient and instead fosters a feeling of positive regard, which means acceptance, appreciation, and respect. And third, he radiates this feeling by visualizing the emotional energy flowing from himself to the recipient. When done properly, this meditation will benefit both the sender and receiver—the sender will be benefited because he will necessarily activate his own heart chakra in order to control his emotions and experience positive regard. Furthermore, his awareness of the sufferings of others will be increased by his effort to serve others, which will also lead to greater compassion. This type of meditation is recommended by *A Course in Miracles,* which emphasizes that "every thought of love you offer...brings you nearer to your wakening to peace eternal and to endless joy."[29]

There are other types of meditation that a person could employ for activating his heart chakra, such as the various devotional practices of bhakti yoga and theistic religions.[30] For an average person, the heart is the next chakra to be developed, and thus it is valuable for him to be involved in some practice that nurtures the quality of compassion within himself.

Consideration of a seed thought is a meditative practice that is part of raja yoga and could be done profitably when in the aesthetic through creative states. The approach is to select a particular seed thought— perhaps a passage of scripture—and then confine one's thinking to that topic during the meditation period. Because a purpose of this effort is deliberately to express the qualities of mental creativity and intuitive wisdom, there should be no mechanical repetition of words, such as in chanting. This type of meditation has three stages: concentration, when the meditator struggles to remain focused on the seed thought and not be distracted by other issues; meditation, when he thinks creatively regarding the seed thought; and contemplation, when he gains intuitive understanding regarding the seed thought. Bailey recommends this approach, but suggests that the person should first use a preliminary step of visualizing a condition of alignment between his physical, emotional, mental, and causal natures.[31] Goldsmith also recommends this type of meditation, but suggests that a person should first read a book of spiritual wisdom until a particular thought attracts his attention— then focus on that thought.[32]

Practicing self-awareness is a meditation that is recommended by Table 8 when in the aesthetic through intuitive states. Ouspensky describes this approach as "self-remembering."[33] Krishnamurti describes it as follows:

> Meditation is to be aware of every thought and of every feeling, never to say it is right or wrong but just to watch it and move with it. In that watching you begin to understand the whole movement of thought and feeling. And out of this awareness comes silence.[34]

This type of meditation is popular among Theravada Buddhists, who call it *Satipatthana,* or "the way of mindfulness." In the Buddhist approach, the meditator endeavors to be aware, or "mindful," of the rise and fall of his abdomen due to breathing. When a break occurs in his attention, he simply notices that it has occurred and how long it has occurred, and then returns his attention back to the rise and fall of his abdomen. When he becomes aware of any feeling, attitude, or thought, he simply acknowledges its presence, and then returns his attention back to the rise and fall of his abdomen.[35]

The practice of self-awareness has two stages. Prior to the development of the brow chakra, the effort is to expand one's consciousness into that of the causal body in order to be detached and objective towards the personality. But after the development of the brow chakra, the effort is to expand one's consciousness into that of the spiritual triad in order to be detached and objective towards the integrated causal body and personality.

Selfless service is another practice listed in Table 8, and it is described by Chaudhuri as "active self-surrender to the Divine."[36] However, much so-called service is misguided, because it is distorted by fanaticism, personal ambition, or illusion. Thus, the effort in this meditation is to perform service in a truly selfless way. If the person has the intention of temporarily ending self-centered activity and instead expressing the spiritual will, and if his brow chakra is developed, then his basic chakra will temporarily become active and transform the kundalini into "the dragon of living fire." The awakened kundalini will then rise to the crown chakra, enabling the latter to register clearly the spiritual will. In other words, this meditation is actually a technique of kundalini yoga.[37]

Some writers indicate that awakening the kundalini requires special postures, breathing exercises, muscle contractions, and deliberate control over interior energies, but these authors are speaking only about an awakening that is premature. If a person needs to use these special methods for awakening the kundalini, then he is attempting to activate his basic chakra before first activating all of his higher ones. However, if his crown chakra is sufficiently active (which means that at least his brow chakra is developed), then he is able to awaken the kundalini simply by choosing to express his spiritual will. But if the brow chakra is not developed, then it is not wise to use special methods for prematurely awakening the kundalini; it is better to practice a meditation that is appropriate for the state of consciousness that has been attained.[38]

In the objective consciousness state, the person experiences the monad indirectly via the spiritual triad. However, he can achieve a still higher state called "monadic consciousness," "sixth initiation," or "Ascension," in which he experiences the monad directly. It is helpful to distinguish between the spiritual will and the monadic will quality. The spiritual will seeks harmonious and right relationships among all beings, whereas the monadic will quality seeks to fulfill the purpose of the one life that expresses itself as all beings. The spiritual will is a reflection on a lower level of the monadic will quality. The last meditation listed in Table 8 is *intense selfless service*. This meditation is appropriate for the objective consciousness state, and it refers to making an effort to directly register and express the monadic will quality.[39]

To summarize, the purpose of meditation is to evoke a quality associated with a state of consciousness higher than one's normal state, with the result of increasing the activity of a center that has not yet been developed. However, this conception of meditation is quite different from that held by many people who think of meditating in terms of becoming as relaxed and comfortable as possible; these people are actually practicing self-hypnosis. The next section will consider self-hypnosis in more detail.

Self-Hypnosis

Bailey relates the trance condition of hypnosis to the experience of "animal sentient life."[40] Hall observes that the human fetus evolves through various animal stages prior to birth, beginning with the fish and then passing to the tortoise, boar, and still higher animal species.[41] There is a sequence of levels for hypnosis that correspond to the sequence of animal stages experienced by a fetus and also to the sequence of unfoldment for the minor etheric chakras. When hypnosis is induced in a human being by any possible means, a lighter or deeper hypnotic trance will occur, depending on how far his consciousness has regressed back into fetal experience. Both self-awareness and spiritual will are absent from all hypnotic levels, corresponding to the fact that these qualities distinguish the human from the animal kingdom. The strength of personality diminishes as the hypnotic trance becomes deeper, corresponding to the fact that different species of animals express varying amounts of what could be called the personality will.

The hypnotic state can be entered in two different directions. First, *a person awakening from sleep will pass from dreamless sleep, through dreaming sleep, through hypnosis, before entering a higher state of consciousness.* Dreaming and hypnosis have the same quality of experience, because the dreamer is awake in his own dream but generally lacks self-awareness. Thus, Table 8 lists dreaming as the meditation for the sleep state.[42] The impulse for awakening is due to the fact that every person has an "instinct to synthesis," which is a basic cause for all expansions of consciousness. Although this instinct is part of his subconscious mind, its origin is higher, because this instinct is actually a reflection of his spiritual will.[43] If this instinct is stronger than the downward pull of any conditioning present in his subconscious mind, then a person on awakening will immediately pass through hypnosis and enter a higher state; this movement is referred to in Table 8 as the meditation for the hypnotic state. But if his conditioning is such that he temporarily abides at the hypnotic level, then somnambulism or sleepwalking could occur.

Second, *a person falling asleep will first pass into hypnosis before reaching the sleep state.* But if he chooses to stop and temporarily abide at the hypnotic level, that is called self-hypnosis. In other words, a person practicing self-hypnosis could be thought of as taking a brief nap, with a limited aspect of himself remaining awake. However, self-hypnosis generally requires a deliberate effort in order to be accomplished.

It is not natural for a human being to abide in a hypnotic trance. Normally, his instinct to synthesis will cause him to enter a higher state; or body fatigue will cause him to enter the sleep state. Consequently, when a hypnotic trance does occur, no matter how it was induced, it is generally only a temporary condition. However, if a person lacks sufficient vitality to properly integrate his dense physical and etheric bodies, he may become stuck in the hypnotic condition. As a result, he may experience a psychotic mental illness such as idiocy, deep depression, obsession, possession, multiple personality, or schizophrenia. In this case, the person's mental illness can often be cured by purely material means that increase his vitality, such as building up his etheric body through sunshine, vitamins, balanced diet, and proper exercise, plus correct treatment and balancing of his endocrine gland system.[44]

A person can choose to employ a variety of methods for accomplishing self-hypnosis, including autosuggestions, repetitive practices, or various systems of blanking and stunning the mind.[45] But why would anyone wish to lower his consciousness and abide in the hypnotic condition? Because there is neither self-awareness nor spiritual will, a hypnotized person can avoid facing his inner mental and emotional conflicts. Because he lacks the ability to question his own thoughts, he can believe suggestions that he would normally disbelieve, and these suggestions could result in his experiencing relaxation, vitality, and happiness. Also, a relaxed condition does help the physical body to recuperate and repair itself. Thus, through self-hypnosis a person can experience a seeming sense of well-being.[46]

A number of "new thought" groups promote self-hypnosis in the form of constant repetition of certain autosuggestions. The person is taught that he is divine and heir of the ages; that any wrong condition, limited circumstance, or unhappy occurrence is the result of his own creative imagination; that these wrong conditions are essentially non-existent; and that by constantly reiterating the affirmed, but unrealized, fact of his divinity, these conditions can be changed. There is some truth in this teaching, because such repetition may eventually change some of the person's circumstances, but without leading to any spiritual growth. Thus, one disadvantage of this approach is that the person remains little better than a self-hypnotized tool of an affirmed, but unrealized, divinity. In contrast, through seeking to understand his conditions, he can become a conscious exponent of that divinity by attaining higher states of consciousness.[47]

Self-hypnosis is generally promoted by religious cults that attempt to "brainwash" or mentally control their subjects. Often the membership as a group is encouraged to chant a particular set of words over and over again, thereby inducing the hypnotic state. In this condition each member is probably happy, has a sense of purpose, and feels secure, while being highly suggestible with respect to the religious beliefs being promulgated. Furthermore, a cult often attempts to structure the rest of each member's day in such a way that he is denied the solitude necessary for reflecting on his thoughts and beliefs. Thus, the strategy of a cult is to encourage self-hypnosis while discouraging true meditation.

Self-hypnosis sometimes occurs when the person deliberately seeks the experience called enlightenment. He may be told that enlightenment can be attained by constantly repeating a particular question to himself, a particular Sanskrit slogan, or some other repetitive task. Because of his greed for enlightenment, the person may fixate on the object of repetition with the effect of falling into a hypnotic trance. Because of his resulting suggestibility, he may experience whatever he conceives enlightenment to be, such as speaking in tongues, seeing a special vision, or receiving a special message. But such an experience is entirely an illusion; the person actually has regressed in consciousness, and he has deceived himself by his own greed.[48]

It is important to conclude this section by emphasizing that the trance condition can be dangerous, because it may open the person to hallucinations, delusions, wrong impressions, or obsessions.[49] Bailey specifically warns against the practice of self-hypnosis: "It is quite easy to induce in oneself an hypnotic condition by the rhythmic repetition of certain words....This is not our object. The trance or automatic condition is dangerous."[50]

Chakra Opening

The term *spiritual development* refers to improving the quality of consciousness, such as increasing compassion, creativity, or intuitiveness; whereas *psychic opening,* as used here, refers to improving communication with the emotional plane. Spiritual development was discussed in earlier sections; psychic opening will be discussed here.

There are two types of etheric webs associated with the major etheric chakras: a) a web blocking the flow of energies between two etheric chakras, which was considered in an earlier section and will be called a development web in this section; and b) a web blocking the flow of energies between an etheric chakra and its emotional counterpart, which will be called an opening web.[51]

When a development web is dissipated, its associated etheric chakra is said to be developed, and when an opening web is dissipated, its associated etheric chakra is said to be opened. Although some books on chakras confuse development with opening, it is important to distinguish clearly between the two. The effect of opening an etheric chakra is to improve communication between it and its counterpart on the emotional plane (sometimes called the astral or psychic plane). As a result, the person's physically focused consciousness can register sense impressions coming from the emotional plane. Leadbeater describes opening webs as follows:

> I have said that the astral and etheric centres are in very close correspondence; but between them, and interpenetrating them in a manner not readily describable, is a sheath or web of closely woven texture, a sheath composed of a single layer of physical atoms much compressed and permeated by a special form of vital force. . . . This web is the protection provided by nature to prevent a premature opening up of communication between the planes.[52]

The common psychic abilities occur by opening the solar plexus chakra and include: clairvoyance, which is seeing images from the emotional plane; and clairaudience, which is hearing sounds from the emotional plane.[53] The opened solar plexus chakra also enables the person to register lower emotions from the emotional plane. The adjective "lower" signifies that these emotions are associated with personal relationships and could be positive or negative in nature. Examples of lower emotions include positive regard, anger, fear, and desire. When the heart chakra is opened, the person is able to register higher emotions from the emotional plane.[54] The adjective "higher" signifies that these latter emotions are associated with group relationships and could also be positive or negative. Examples of higher emotions include compassion, devotion, and a consciousness of the weight of grief under which humanity struggles. And when the crown chakra is opened, the person is said to be an "illumined seer" and can register an "inflow of light, information and inspiration," which is a higher form of clairvoyance and clairaudience.[55]

Two different types of out-of-body experiences have been described. The first type is called *astral projection* and occurs via the opened solar plexus chakra. Here the person, while in a hypnotic trance, is able to function in his emotional body on the emotional plane. However, there may be no relation between the person's physical plane existence and the out-of-body experiences which he can relate while in a trance and of which he often remains unaware in his normal waking consciousness.[56] The second type, which is a higher form, is called *samadhi* and occurs via the opened crown chakra. Samadhi is a Sanskrit word meaning "self-aware conscious union with Spirit." The withdrawal in samadhi is consciously undertaken, and at no point is the person in trance, unconscious, or asleep. In fact, to accomplish samadhi, the kundalini energy must first be awakened and raised to the crown chakra. Because the physical brain remains alert, whatever is contacted or known during this process becomes part of the brain's memory, so that there is "continuity of consciousness" between physical and out-of-body experience.[57]

Following the development of the brow chakra, the basic chakra can be temporarily activated. As a result, the kundalini energy can be temporarily transformed into "the dragon of living fire," which then surges up the spine to reach the crown chakra. One effect of awakening the kundalini is to open the solar plexus, heart, and crown chakras, implying that the person can experience all of the psychic abilities that were previously described, although considerable practice may be needed to use those abilities with skill and accuracy.[58] Consequently, some authors associate psychic powers with the brow chakra. However, as stated earlier, the common psychic abilities actually occur via opening the solar plexus chakra.

Prior to the development of the brow chakra, it is possible to practice certain techniques that can lead to opening the solar plexus chakra. A number of books have been published that describe these techniques, which are often a combination of breathing exercise, special posture, self-hypnosis, and visualization. In this way, a person could develop such abilities as clairvoyance, clairaudience, and astral projection. But in this case the opening of the solar plexus chakra would be premature, because he would lack the emotional stability, mental control, and intuitive understanding needed for safely and wisely using the associated psychic abilities.[59]

There are also a number of commercial "mind-training" courses that advertise the attainment of various psychic powers. Almost all these courses use a heavy dose of hypnotic programming, although the term "hypnosis" may be denied and instead be called "brain-wave training" or "alpha training." In addition to the psychic abilities already mentioned, these courses generally teach how to develop, or obtain, a psychic adviser who can be contacted within a deep level of the mind and who can then offer guidance. Unfortunately, the person may consider the adviser as being divine, thus leading to blind and unquestioning acceptance of the offered guidance. But such acceptance can create many problems, including mediumistic possession.[60]

A person with premature psychic opening may have difficulty in correctly interpreting what he sees and hears on the emotional plane. Perhaps he is just abstracting the content of his own subconscious mind. Or, he may be receiving teachings from discarnate entities who are relatively unevolved. Or, he may be unable to differentiate the sensed images and sounds between that which is past, present, and future. Or, he may be tuning in on the forebodings of other people while believing that those forebodings refer to his own coming experience.[61] Or, he may be contacting an "astral thoughtform" of a famous being, such as Jesus, while believing that an actual visitation is occurring.[62] Consequently, a psychic may be greatly deceived and be deceiving others, even while honestly reporting exactly what he experiences.

A person with premature psychic opening may encounter additional difficulties. He may gain greater vanity by believing that his powers demonstrate his superiority over others. He may lack control over his powers and be unable to stop seeing or hearing psychic phenomena, no matter how hard he tries to stop. His life may become more complex, because he is living simultaneously on the physical and emotional planes. He may experience nervous tension, brain disturbance, and debility. He may experience obsession, temporary or permanent. He may eventually be placed in a sanitarium or asylum, because he has become unfit for normal living. His plight may be made more extreme by lack of understanding from his friends, and from any consulting physicians or psychologists. Proper handling of such a case would be based upon recognizing that these troubles are not mental in origin, but are entirely related to the solar plexus chakra.[63]

Bailey also cautions against being entangled with the psychic experiences of an opened solar plexus chakra. If this chakra has been opened prematurely, she recommends that it be closed in the following way: by ceasing to practice any breathing exercise, posture, or other method that may have led to opening the solar plexus chakra; by ceasing to be interested in the display of psychic powers; by controlling emotion, because emotion serves to keep the "door ajar"; by following a course of intellectual training and mental development; and by emphasizing higher goals including a life of service.[64]

Admonitions

This chapter has given several admonitions to the reader, and it may be useful to summarize them in the order presented:

- Refrain from deliberately attempting to dissipate the development webs;
- Refrain from concentrating upon a chakra during meditation;
- Refrain from prematurely attempting to awaken the kundalini;
- Refrain from practicing self-hypnosis; and
- Refrain from prematurely attempting to develop psychic powers.

Chapter 4

Pranic Healing

This chapter will examine how prana, sometimes called vitality or magnetism, can be used to purify and stimulate the chakras within the patient's etheric body. Throughout this chapter the word *chakra* will be used to refer only to an etheric force center and not to a center on a higher plane.

Prana

Prana is a Sanskrit word derived from *pra,* meaning "forth," and the verb root *an,* "to breathe." Thus, *prana* means "to breathe forth," and it refers to the "life breath" or "life force" that vitalizes the etheric body and nervous system. Yogi Ramacharaka gives the following definition: "Prana is the Force by which all activity is carried on in the body—by which all bodily movements are possible—by which all functioning is done—by which all signs of life manifest themselves."[1] A comparison can be made between prana, the active power producing all vital phenomena, and oxygen, the active chemical agent and supporter of combustion in all organic life.[2]

Chapter 1 defined the sutratma to be the life stream coming from the monad and going to the heart chakra, where it is anchored during the life cycle. This life stream is different from prana, and the following distinctions can be made between the functions of these two energies.

Table 9. Differentiation of Prana, According to Various Sources*

Type	Traditional definition	Bailey	Leadbeater
Prana	"It controls our breathing, and enables us to draw in the universal Life-forces into our physical being."	"Prana, extending from the nose to the heart and having special relation to the mouth and speech, the heart and lungs."	"The yellow ray is directed to the heart, but after doing its work there part of it also passes on to the brain."
Vyana	"The life-breath which governs the circulations in the body and hence is that which . . . keeps the body in shape."	"Its instruments are the thousands of nadis or nerves found in the body; and it has a peculiar definite connection with the blood channels, the veins and arteries."	"The rose-coloured ray runs all over the body along the nerves, and is clearly the life of the nervous system."
Samana	"The life-breath which controls digestion and assimilation, and hence is that which carries on the chemical processes."	"Samana extends from the heart to the solar plexus; it concerns food and the nourishing of the body."	"The green ray floods the abdomen, and while centring especially in the solar plexus, evidently vivifies . . . the digestive apparatus generally."
Apana	"The life-breath which casts out of the human system all that is waste material, the death force of the lower part of the body."	"Apana controls from the solar plexus to the soles of the feet; it concerns the organs of elimination, of rejection and of birth."	"The orange-red ray flows to the base of the spine and thence to the generative organs."
Upana	"The life-breath which directs the vital currents of the body upward to their sources, to the higher centers of their being."	"Upana is found between the nose and the top of the head; it has a special relation to the brain, the nose and the eyes."	"The violet-blue ray flashes upwards to the throat, where it seems to divide itself, the light blue remaining . . . , while the dark blue and violet pass on into the brain."

*The traditional definitions in the second column of this table come from The Language of the Gods, by J. M. Tyberg, pages 102-103. The Bailey definitions are from her work entitled The Light of the Soul, pages 329-330; and Leadbeater's definitions come from his book, The Chakras, pages 55-61. For full publication data, the reader is referred to the Bibliography.

The life stream holds in coherency the integrated physical body, whereas prana vitalizes the individual atoms and cells. The life stream controls the circulation of prana in the etheric body as well as the circulation of blood in the dense physical body.[3]

Prana is generally understood to originate as emanations from the sun that are later absorbed by the splenic chakra. Leadbeater has a similar perspective but believes that prana takes the form of certain atoms, called "vitality globules," that have been vitalized or charged by a solar force; these vitality globules are able to flow into a person's splenic center and then gradually transfer their vitality to the chakras and nervous system.[4]

According to yoga philosophy, prana differentiates into five types within the human body: prana, vyana, samana, apana, and upana.[5] Bailey also gives this same fivefold differentiation for prana.[6] Both the traditional Sanskrit definitions and Bailey's descriptions for the five types are listed in Table 9, and it can be seen that Bailey is consistent with the traditional viewpoint.

On the other hand, Leadbeater states that after vitality globules are received and assimilated by the splenic center, they are split into seven different types or colors. Presumably based on his own paranormal observations, Leadbeater describes the seven colors as follows: yellow, rose red, green, orange, dark red, violet and blue. But after leaving the splenic center, the violet and blue join into one ray, and so do the orange and dark red. Thus, Leadbeater considers that the vitality actually flows through the body in five main streams, which he then identifies with the five traditional differentiations of prana.[7] As can be seen from Table 9, Leadbeater's and Bailey's descriptions for the five types are in general agreement.

However, the colors observed by Leadbeater should be thought of as only symbolic. Although a clairvoyant may in all sincerity believe that he has registered a color or a series of colors, there is actually no color present. What he has really contacted is an impression of vibrational quality that his mind and brain rapidly translate into the symbology of color.[8] Several clairvoyants receiving the same impressions might actually see different colors if they have different associations for the symbols.

Later Powell carefully read Leadbeater's description of the pranic flow through the body and constructed the diagram in Figure 3 to

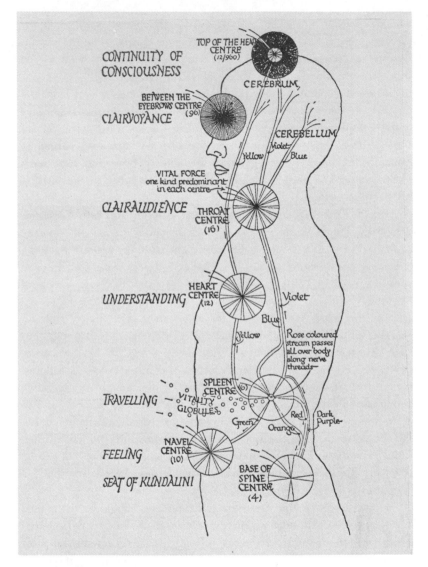

Figure 3. Man and His Etheric Centres. This is a reproduction of page 56 from A.E. Powell's *The Etheric Double,* first published in 1925 and reprinted in 1978 by the Theosophical Publishing House, Wheaton, IL. In this original illustration, the numbers in parentheses relate to the number of "petals" in the corresponding chakra. The reader should note that the terms used by Powell for the role of each chakra—Continuity of Consciousness, Clairvoyance, Clairaudience, Understanding, Travelling, Feeling and Seat of Kundalini—are in some cases different from the roles assigned in the previous chapter.

summarize this process. This diagram illustrates how vitality globules are first absorbed by the splenic chakra, differentiated into seven and then five streams, and then sent to vitalize the other chakras. This diagram refers to the solar plexus as the "navel centre" and does not include the sacral chakra.

For the purposes of the present study, it is not necessary to understand in detail how prana differentiates and flows through the etheric body. But there is an important point made by Table 9 and Figure 3 that is useful to remember: the type of specialized prana used to vitalize one chakra may not be the same as that used to vitalize another.

Treatment of Chakras

As discussed in Chapter 2, an important function of the chakras is to vitalize the dense physical body, including the endocrine glands. From this point of view, disease can begin as a poor condition in one or more of the chakras, which then affects the activity of the nadis. Chapter 2 described the nadis as a system of etheric channels or tiny threads of force that underlie the nervous system. Thus, activity in the nadis affects the nervous system, which in turn affects the glandular system and hormones sent by the blood throughout the body. In this way a poor condition in the chakras translates into a poor condition in the dense physical body.[9]

It is the approach of pranic healing to heal the physical body by directing prana to one or more of the etheric chakras. The idea is that stimulating a chakra in this manner also will vitalize the associated body organs and endocrine glands. Table 3 shows the relationships between the etheric chakras and organs, and Table 5 shows the relationships with the glands. Using Table 3, it is possible to identify the chakra associated with a diseased organ. For example, if the patient's problem is related to his liver, then his solar plexus chakra should be treated; or if the patient is suffering from difficulty in his lungs, then his throat chakra should be treated.

Because a malfunctioning chakra may be either underactive or overactive, there are two types of treatment for it:

Stimulation. If the chakra vitalizing the diseased area of the physical body is diagnosed as being underactive, then pranic energy can be sent to stimulate that chakra into greater activity.

Abstraction. If the chakra vitalizing the diseased area is diagnosed as being overactive, then prana can be sent to stimulate a higher chakra in order to reduce the activity of the lower one. In the course of evolution, the heart center will control the solar plexus, throat will control the sacral, brow will control the heart and throat, and crown will control the brow and basic. Thus, for example, if the sacral center is viewed as being overactive, then prana should be sent to vitalize the throat center in order to abstract energy from the sacral.[10]

Pranic healing employs the planetary etheric body as the medium linking the healer with the patient. There is no reality to separation, because the healer's and the patient's etheric bodies are integral parts of the planetary etheric body, which is whole, unbroken, and continuous. In other words, there does exist an etheric cord that connects the healer with the patient, even though they may be separated by hundreds of miles. When they are separated, which is the case called "absent healing," it is necessary for the healer to establish a rapport with the patient. The feeling of positive regard, which includes acceptance, appreciation, and respect, can produce the necessary rapport. Thus, before sending any prana, the healer first should momentarily send positive regard, which serves to vitalize an etheric cord linking his etheric body to the patient's.[11]

After the patient has been properly diagnosed and one of his centers has been identified for stimulation, the next step is for the healer to send prana to that center. The discussion in the preceding section suggests that a patient's chakra may be receptive to prana coming only from the corresponding chakra belonging to the healer, as this may be the healer's only chakra using the same specialized type of prana. Accordingly, the healer should have the concept that there exists a channel, or a vitalized etheric cord, along which health-giving prana can be sent from the "needed center" in his etheric body to the corresponding center in the body of the patient.[12]

How does the healer send this prana? The term *conscious mind* refers to the combination of the consciousness stream (enabling the person to have self-awareness), mental body, and physical brain. It should be remembered that the etheric body is part of the physical. Just as the conscious mind can direct movements of the dense physical body, the mind also can direct energy movements of the etheric physical body. As repeatedly emphasized by Bailey, a fundamental and universal law is that "energy follows thought."[13] The point is that the healer, merely through mental direction, is able to send currents of prana to the patient, provided that a linking etheric cord has been vitalized.

To avoid becoming depleted, the healer must draw extra prana into his own etheric body in order to replace that being sent to the patient. How can this extra prana be drawn in? Although prana is not absorbed through the lungs, its intake is associated with breathing. The breathing motion induces activity in the splenic chakra, which in turn absorbs prana from the atmosphere. Deep rhythmic breathing enables more prana to be assimilated than does shallow or irregular breathing. However, the healer may not need to change his breathing deliberately to draw in additional prana, because his subconscious mind may automatically change the breathing pattern for him.[14]

The prana sent by the healer includes more than just pure prana or vitality. It is important to realize that this prana will be qualified by the forces acting within the healer's etheric body. Because the etheric body is a focus point for all interior energies, this prana will be affected by forces coming from the healer's emotional apparatus, mind, and causal body. Consequently, it is very important that the healer have emotional poise and mental clarity when sending pranic energy, so that the forces qualifying this energy are therapeutic for the patient.[15]

In summary, the prana that is absorbed by the healer goes through a two-stage transformation process before being sent: it is first differentiated by the splenic center into the divisions given in Table 9; and after the specialized prana reaches a major chakra, it is then qualified by the forces acting on that chakra.

What is the effect of this energy on the patient? Healing work is circulatory. After the pranic energy is directed by thought to a patient's chakra, it does not accumulate at that chakra. Rather, the prana passes through the chakra and then through the nadis, nervous system, associated endocrine gland, and diseased organ, before affecting the rest of the dense physical body. This process could be regarded as a system of "flushing," with a purificatory and stimulating effect.[16]

The following analogy can be made with respect to food. If a weak person loses the power to digest food, the remedy is to prepare food already partially digested that can be assimilated by his stomach. Similarly, if a person is unable to draw in and specialize prana for himself, he may still be able to absorb what has been already prepared by another and so gain the strength needed to resume the normal functioning of his organs.[17]

Modes of Distribution

The healer does not necessarily send prana directly from his chakra to the corresponding chakra of the patient; instead this energy may first go to another of the healer's centers that acts as a distribution point. Three different chakras have been identified as being possible distribution points—the splenic, solar plexus, and brow.

First consider the case in which the healer distributes specialized prana via his own splenic chakra. There need not be any chakra unfoldment to use this center, because all minor chakras, including the splenic, are considered to be developed at birth. To ensure that the prana is therapeutically qualified, the healer should have "physical purity," obtained through control of sexual expression, careful eating, and proper physical exercise. Bailey describes splenic distribution as follows:

> It is this prana which is distributed or transferred by a natural healer (one without any training, without much essential knowledge or with little, if any, spiritual orientation). He heals but does not know how or why; prana simply flows through him in the form of a strong current of animal vitality, usually from the splenic centre and not from any of the seven centres.[18]

Next consider the case in which the healer distributes specialized prana via his solar plexus chakra, which requires that this chakra be developed. In order for the prana to be therapeutically qualified, the healer should have "emotional purity," referring to control of the desire nature. Naylor gives the following description for this type of distribution, where the term "Third Eye" refers to the brow chakra: "Most of this [prana] comes from the solar plexus and radiates from here rather than the Third Eye. It spreads out through the hands if you so direct it."[19] This indicates that prana can be focused with the hands, referring to the minor hand chakras listed in Table 4. By employing the hand chakras in this way, the healer is able to focus the prana directly at the receiving chakra in the patient's etheric body. Prana can be viewed as a wavelike phenomenon, and a hand chakra as a focusing lens.

In the final case, the healer directs and distributes specialized prana via his brow chakra, which requires that this chakra be developed. In order for the prana to be appropriately qualified, the healer should have "mental purity," which refers to understanding the essential divinity of a human being. Chaney gives the following description for brow distribution:

> Once a disciple stimulates the Third Eye, he automatically becomes a healer. ... He can create a tremendous power which, flowing from his brow into the hands and on outward along the etheric cord to reach the patient, can effect a miraculous and instantaneous healing.[20]

This indicates that the hand chakras can focus prana coming from the brow, just as Naylor indicated that the hands can focus energy coming from the solar plexus. The hands also can focus prana coming from the splenic chakra.

What is the advantage of distributing prana via the brow chakra, rather than by the first two methods? Bailey gives the following answer: "All the centres in the body of the patient can be receptive to this energy, and not just one, as in the previous two types of healing."[21] Thus, only one of the major chakras can be "receptive" to specialized prana distributed via either the splenic or solar plexus chakra, whereas all centers can be receptive to prana distributed via the brow chakra. In particular, both the patient's splenic chakra (considered to be a minor center) and sacral chakra (considered to be a major center) can be receptive to specialized prana from the healer's splenic chakra that is distributed via this chakra. The patient's solar plexus chakra can be receptive to specialized prana from the healer's solar plexus chakra that is distributed via this chakra. But any of the patient's chakras can be receptive to specialized prana extracted from the healer's corresponding center, after being distributed via the latter's brow chakra.

As stated in Chapter 3, the highest chakra developed in an "average" person is the solar plexus. Consequently, the preceding discussion implies that only two types of specialized prana can be distributed by an average person, namely, that specialized for the splenic and solar plexus chakras. On the other hand, Leadbeater identifies only two types of energy that can be readily distributed by a healer: "rose-coloured vitality," which he considers to be prana specialized for the splenic chakra; and "nerve-ether," which he considers to be a "fluid which keeps up the constant circulation of etheric matter along the nerves."[22] According to Chapter 2, one of the functions of the solar plexus chakra is to vitalize the sympathetic nervous system. If Leadbeater's nerve-ether is the same as prana specialized for the solar plexus chakra, then his viewpoint is consistent with the preceding discussion.

The patient's intention controls the activity of his own chakras. Thus, in any mode of esoteric healing, effective results generally require that the patient requests the assistance, trusts the healer, and truly wishes to be healed in order for the patient's chakras to be receptive to the healer's influence.[23] Whether developed or undeveloped, a chakra has the important function of using prana to vitalize a portion of the dense physical body. Consequently, the patient is able to respond to treatment with prana irrespective of his chakra development, provided that he has become properly receptive.

Role of a Higher Intelligence

As discussed earlier, the pranic healer attempts either to stimulate or to abstract energy from one or more of a patient's chakras. In either case, the practitioner would be well advised to move with caution in determining which centers should be treated and how they should be treated, because serious mistakes could be made. It is better to have no effect on the patient than to make a mistake, such as suddenly stimulating a center that is already overactive or abstracting energy from a depleted center. Consequently, before proceeding with pranic healing, it is important that the patient be carefully diagnosed.[24]

Rather than the healer making these diagnostic decisions himself, another alternative has been offered by several writers: the healer can invoke the assistance of a higher intelligence. For example, Bailey refers to the role of a "Master" or a "Master's group,"[25] Edwards to "spirit doctors" or "Spirit healing intelligences,"[26] and Meek to "discarnate entities."[27] However, Bailey indicates that the healer must have earned the right to call on such assistance on behalf of the patient.[28] Presumably, this right is earned through the healer's dedication, persistence, and purification. In other words, not every healer who invokes this assistance will receive it.

If the assistance of the higher intelligence has been both earned and invoked, then this intelligence is able to make the right diagnostic decisions as well as direct the needed energies for any form of pranic healing:

Contact healing. In this case the practitioner is present with the patient. His first step is to help the patient relax. Next, if he slowly passes his hands along one side of the patient's dense physical body, he can experience a signal from the higher intelligence as a heat, coldness, or "tingling" in his hands, thereby identifying an area (representing a major or minor chakra) that should be treated. After such a signal has been noted, the healer should allow the pranic force to flow through his hands to the designated area, with both hands placed about three inches from the body surface. When the healer senses that the pranic force has been "turned off," he should again continue to pass his hands along the patient's body until another signal is received, or until both back and front sides have been entirely scanned. Most of the major chakras are behind the body, and most of the minor ones are in front. When following this procedure, the healer need not have any knowledge of chakra locations, except for the one rule that the hands be placed about three inches from the body surface. This particular distance is recommended because for an average person it is the approximate interval between the dense spine and a major spinal chakra.[29]

Absent healing. In this case the healer is at a distance from the patient, and his first step is establishing a rapport by momentarily sending feelings of positive regard, which vitalize an etheric cord linking his etheric body to the patient's. Then he need only allow the higher intelligence to direct the pranic flows, using his brow, solar plexus, or splenic center as a distribution point.

This work could be thought of as a collaboration: the healer needs the higher intelligence to diagnose the patient and direct the appropriate energies, and the higher intelligence needs the healer's etheric body to assimilate prana and convert this prana into healing force. After this higher intelligence is invoked, the healer need not deliberately direct the energy movements. Although energy flows in the etheric body are generally below the threshold of consciousness, the healer can nevertheless experience physiological changes and in this way know that he is transmitting prana. For example, he may experience a spontaneous change in his breathing, pulsating vibrations in his body, and a pressure in his head area. This change in breathing and these vibrations enable the healer's etheric body to draw in new prana to replace that being sent. A pressure in the head area indicates the use of the brow center for distribution.

When the higher intelligence directs the energy movements, the practitioner need not have any technical knowledge about the locations and functions of the chakras, although such knowledge may be useful in understanding the experiences that both he and the patient undergo. This circumstance explains why there are a number of books giving instruction in the art of healing that do not mention the chakras at all but describe how to become a channel for this higher intelligence. If the healer has become such a channel, then he can choose to regain control at any moment, either to terminate the process or to select the energies that are being sent.

Whether the healer or higher intelligence directs the energy flows, the work will be limited by the healer's chakra development, as described in the previous section. Nevertheless, there usually will be better results when under the direction of the higher intelligence, because this intelligence has greater knowledge of energy flows in the etheric body and therefore can exercise more accurate mental control over these flows.

Effectiveness of Healing

It may be useful to summarize the preceding information by tracing the flow of prana from the sun, via the healer, to the patient. Let us suppose that the patient has difficulty with his lungs; according to Table 3, the patient's throat center should be stimulated. Let us suppose also that the healer is able to use his brow center to distribute prana. The steps are as follows:

1. The healer's **splenic chakra** assimilates pranic radiations from the sun and then differentiates this prana into five streams of specialized vitality that are sent to vivify the other chakras.

2. Some of this specialized prana reaches the healer's **throat chakra,** where it is qualified by the various forces acting on that center.

3. The healer draws some of this energy up to his head, where it is directed through his **brow chakra** to the patient.

4. The healer may or may not wish to use the minor centers in the **hands** to focus the energy.

5. After the prana reaches the patient's **throat chakra,** it has a purificatory and stimulating effect on that center, the thyroid gland, the lungs, and the body as a whole.

After all of these steps, will the patient's health improve? Often the answer is yes, but the results may be only temporary. Chapter 1 stated that physical disease can have either an external or an internal cause. If it has an internal cause, this cause can be at the etheric, emotional, or mental level. Table 2 listed some etheric and emotional conditions that may result in physical illness. If the cause were at the emotional or mental level, then a poor condition in the etheric chakras would merely be a reflection of a deeper and more fundamental problem, so pranic healing would be treating only symptoms. In that case, the best that treatment with prana can accomplish is to produce a temporary abatement of the disease but not a permanent cure.[30]

The next two chapters will discuss telepathic and radiatory healing, methods that may allow harmony to be established on deeper levels.

Chapter 5

Telepathic Healing

Although telepathy literally means "feeling at a distance," the term is used here to mean the transfer of any cognitive impulse from one person to another while utilizing the etheric subplanes as the linking medium of communication. This chapter will examine the relationships between telepathy and the etheric chakras, as well as the application of telepathy to healing.

Telepathy

Perhaps the following examples will clarify the concept of a communication medium. Written words can be conveyed on a solid medium, such as paper, and then be registered with the eye. Sound waves can be transmitted through a liquid medium, such as an ocean, and then be registered with sonar equipment. Sound waves also can be transmitted through a gaseous medium, the air, and then be registered with the ear. As described in this chapter, telepathic impulses can be transmitted via the etheric subplanes and then be registered with an etheric chakra. And psychic opening enables communication to take place via the emotional plane and then be registered with an emotional chakra followed by an opened etheric chakra. (Psychic opening was briefly considered in Chapter 3.)

There are two important statements that should be made regarding telepathy. First, *the planetary etheric body is the medium of telepathic communication.* Jurriaanse gives the following description for this process:

> Once the concept of the etheric system is accepted and understood, then the basic principles which govern the functioning of telepathy can also be readily grasped. Because this vital energy vehicle interpenetrates and interrelates *all* that exist on our planet—and the Universe—impulses that are sent forth on etheric waves will vibrate and circulate throughout the entire etheric world.[1]

Second, *each type of telepathic impulse is sent or received with an etheric chakra.* Bailey has related telepathy to the etheric chakras, and her discussion is outlined in Table 10, where five types of impulses are distinguised: intuitions, concrete thoughts, higher emotions, lower emotions, and sensual. For each type of impulse, this table lists the corresponding etheric chakra that acts as a transmitting or receiving antenna.

A person also has force centers in his mental and emotional bodies that are counterparts of those in his etheric body. Consequently, it may seem surprising that his etheric chakras are used to transmit and receive telepathic impulses of a mental or emotional nature. Instead it might be thought that his mental chakras would be utilized for mental impulses, and his emotional chakras for emotional impulses. But while a person is on the physical plane, the main purpose of his mental and emotional centers is to convey energies between his own inner vehicles, rather than to communicate with another person. However, psychic communication does employ the emotional chakras to transmit and receive impulses via the emotional plane; but even in this case, the received psychic impressions must be passed down to the physical body, via an opened etheric chakra, in order to be registered by the receiver's physically focused consciousness. Because telepathy employs the etheric chakras to transmit and receive impulses via the etheric medium, the remainder of this chapter will use the word *chakra* to refer only to an etheric force center and not to a force center on a higher plane.

Chapter 1 stated that the mental plane can be divided into two categories: an abstract portion corresponding to the three highest subplanes and a concrete portion corresponding to the four lowest subplanes. Similarly, two types of mental impulses can be sent and received: intuitions associated with the causal body in the abstract portion, and concrete thoughts associated with the mental body in the concrete portion. The term *intuition* refers to an abstract or nonverbal understanding of some idea.

Table 10. Relation between Etheric Chakras and Telepathy*

Type of Impression	Chakra Used In Transmission	Chakra Used In Reception	Description
Intuitions	Crown and brow	Crown	"That form of communi- cation which has been responsible for . . . inspirational writings of real power."
Concrete thoughts	Throat and solar plexus	Throat and solar plexus	"This is the activity and rapport established from mind to mind."
Higher emotions	Heart	Heart	"High and consecrated feeling, devotion, aspira- tion and love."
Lower emotions	Solar plexus	Solar plexus	"It concerns emotions (fear, hate, disgust, love, desire and many other purely astral reactions)."
Sensual	(not avail- able from Bailey)	Sacral	"Such impacting impres- sions . . . will have reference to all that concerns his physical being, his physical ap- petites, and his physical comfort or discomfort."

*The source for this material is Alice Bailey's *Telepathy and the Etheric Vehicle,* first published in 1950 and reprinted in 1975 by the Lucis Publishing Company, New York.

First consider intuitional telepathy. The intuitions begin with the transmitter's causal body, are passed down first to his crown and then to his brow chakra, are transmitted by his brow chakra over etheric vibratory waves, and finally are registered by the receiver's crown chakra. The brow chakra is not used for reception. This process could be called "formless telepathy," because the transmission as well as registration is wordless and formless. The recipient gains a nonverbal or intuitive understanding of the communicated ideas, although he may later wish to use his mental body and throat center for formulating and expressing those ideas as concrete thoughts and words.[2]

The mental body is linked to the physical brain via the emotional body, solar plexus chakra, and then throat chakra. Thus, the etheric representations of concrete thoughts are actually in the form of "emotions which can be registered by the image-making faculty of the mind."[3] In the case of mental telepathy, the solar plexus chakra is used for both transmission and reception. The concrete thoughts begin with the transmitter's mental body, are transmitted by his solar plexus chakra over etheric waves, are first received by the receiver's solar plexus chakra, and are finally registered by the receiver's throat chakra and physical brain.[4]

Emotions also can be differentiated into two categories: higher emotions, such as compassion and devotion, which refer to group relationships; and lower emotions, such as positive regard, anger, fear, and desire, which refer to individual relationships. Both types of emotions can be transmitted over the etheric medium—the higher emotions are transmitted from heart chakra to heart chakra,[5] whereas the lower emotions are transmitted from solar plexus chakra to solar plexus chakra.[6] Lower emotional communication via the solar plexus is often instinctive and is currently the most prevalent type of telepathy. For instance, this process occurs when a mother "feels" that some danger threatens her child, or that some happening is taking place in connection with her child.

The final category listed in Table 10 is sensual impulses, referring to physical comfort or discomfort, hunger, lust, and so forth. Bailey states that these impressions are registered by the sacral chakra, but she did not indicate the chakra used for transmission.[7] However, the splenic chakra is probably the transmitter for sensual impulses—

Chapter 4 indicated that this chakra can distribute specialized prana, and there is a close connection between prana and telepathy.

Telepathic communication is related to psychic abilities in the sense that the chakras play similar roles in both cases. For example, intuitional telepathy is related to samadhi, because the later is experienced via the opened crown chakra. Mental telepathy is related to clairaudience, because the latter is first received via the opened solar plexus chakra and then registered by the throat chakra and physical brain.

It is useful to distinguish between positive regard and compassion, although the word "love" is sometimes used to denote either one. Positive regard is a feeling of acceptance, appreciation, and respect for another person; while compassion, as the word is being used here, means to have an intuitive perception of the essential nonseparateness of human beings. Positive regard relates to another person, while compassion relates to humanity as a whole. Positive regard is experienced via the solar plexus chakra, while compassion is experienced via the heart chakra. Having positive regard is facilitated by first having compassion, and one can think of positive regard as the result of "stepping down" compassion to the level of individual relationships.[8]

In any form of telepathy, the feeling of positive regard can be the coherent factor linking together the transmitter and receiver. Thus, the transmitter should first establish a rapport by momentarily sending positive regard to the receiver, before sending a desired idea, thought, or image.[9] As discussed in Chapter 4, positive regard plays a similar role in linking the healer to patient when sending pranic energy.

Successful telepathic communication requires appropriate development of the chakras belonging to both sender and receiver; but none of these centers need be opened, because the medium of telepathic communication is the etheric and not the emotional plane. Due to lack of development, a transmitter may not have the capacity to send certain types of messages, or it may happen that a transmitter is able to send a message that cannot be registered by the recipient. The chakra development necessary for successful telepathic interaction will be described later in this chapter.

In addition to Bailey's discussion relating telepathy to the chakras, the viewpoints of some other writers are worthy of consideration.

Besant considers the pineal gland to be the organ for sending and receiving thoughts by way of the etheric medium.[10] By examining Table 5, it can be seen that the pineal gland is associated with the crown chakra. Ball associates the throat chakra with the ability to transmit mental messages.[11] Chaney suggests using a vigorous breathing exercise that "awakens the solar plexus chakra, resulting in telepathy."[12] Thus, other sources corroborate, at least to some degree, the roles assigned by Bailey to the crown, throat, and solar plexus chakras.

The preceding discussion emphasized the relationship between telepathy and chakras, but the actual practice of telepathy need not require the conscious direction of any chakra. If an experienced worker has the requisite chakra development and abides in the highest state of consciousness that he has attained, then his entire chakra system will automatically implement his desired intention.[13] A good analogy is ordinary speech. After learning how to vocalize, a person speaks merely by intending to do so, and the needed coordination of muscles and nerves takes place automatically. And so it is with telepathy, as neither broadcaster nor receiver need be concerned with deliberately directing the etheric centers.

With what, then, should the broadcaster and receiver be concerned in order to have successful telepathic work? Following are three suggestions:

1. There should be no emotional barriers between transmitter and receiver, such as criticism or suspicion.

2. The transmitter should momentarily send the feeling of positive regard to the receiver in order to establish a rapport, but afterward the transmitter should be occupied mainly with the clarity of his message, which may consist of intuitive ideas, concrete thoughts, or symbolic pictures.

3. The receiver should momentarily send positive regard to the transmitter, which also establishes a rapport, and afterward the receiver needs to have a casual and detached attitude while being receptive to any external ideas, thoughts, or mental images.[14]

Healing of Mental Attitudes

The first application of telepathy to esoteric healing is transmitting certain therapeutic ideas to the mind of a recipient. These ideas may have the effect of changing the receiver's point of view, outlook on life, or technique of living.

Consider first what the telepathic worker should *not* do. Because the image held of another will tend to strengthen the corresponding qualities (whether good or evil) in that person, great care should be used when thinking about someone else. In particular, one should avoid all criticism or condemnation of another's defects, for that judgment will tend to strengthen those very flaws.[15]

When telepathically sending help, one should never attempt to interfere with another's free choice. Besant makes the point that "no man should try to impose his will on another, even in order to make him do right."[16] Indeed, an effort to force an issue or to bring mental pressure is a form of "black magic" that may weaken the recipient.

Next consider what can be done. It is possible to send helpful ideas telepathically to someone without any sense of imposition or compulsion. This can occur if the transmitter's intention is sufficiently pure, so that the effort is only to offer ideas for consideration rather than to impose them. The ideas to be offered should be selected with great care. They should be unquestionable and unchanging philosophic truths, noncompulsive and wholly beneficent in their influence and clearly understood by the transmitter.[17]

The following are possible ideas that could be transmitted: "separation is a thing of the past and...unity is the goal of the immediate future"; or "hatred is retro-active and undesirable and...goodwill is the touchstone which will transform the world."[18] But always the recipient is allowed the freedom to accept or reject whatever thoughts are sent.

This type of work is more potent when an entire group acts as the impressing agent. Bailey gives the following steps for such a group to use when directing ideas to some individual:

1. The stage of pondering over the idea which is to be impressed upon the mind of some individual. This pondering and careful directed thinking produces *construction.*

2. When the thoughtform is thus built in your mind, there will follow a period wherein it comes alive. It slowly becomes the living embodiment of the desired idea— vibrant, active and ready for service.

3. When this stage is reached, you can then—as a group— proceed with the stage of direction. Having carefully in mind the person to be impressed and the fact of your group as the impressing agent (thus providing the two poles between which interplay is desired), you will try to see the living embodied idea, playing back and forth between the two poles. You will send it out on the wings of love, impelled by the wise desire to serve. [19]

How does this work relate to the chakras? To accomplish intuitional telepathy, the transmitter should have his brow chakra developed to send intuitions from that chakra, and the receiver should have his throat chakra developed to register these intuitions with his crown chakra. [20] To accomplish mental telepathy, both the transmitter and receiver should have their solar plexus chakras developed and their throat chakras sufficiently active. [21] If the transmitter has sufficient development, he should endeavor to embody his message with both intuitional and mental impulses and then allow the receiver to register whatever his own development permits.

Healing of Physical Diseases

A telepathic worker also can endeavor to bring about a physical healing. The underlying theory here is that there are three different levels of mind that can affect the health of the physical body: the conscious mind (which has been considered previously); the subconscious mind (which controls and manages the operations of every organ and cell); and the cellular mind (which is the consciousness of an individual cell of the body).

The subconscious mind functions below the threshold of consciousness and operates through the five lower chakras, nervous system, and endocrine glands, with the solar plexus chakra acting as an important control station. This mind constantly supervises the work of digestion, elimination, circulation, etc., which require that the activity of the many organs and cells be coordinated. Each cell has a mental aspect that demonstrates through instinctive knowledge, adaptation, and memory. The consciousness of each cell, although rudimentary, is sufficiently evolved to accomplish that cell's work. The attitudes and beliefs adopted by the conscious mind can influence the subconscious mind, which in turn controls the cellular minds.[22]

The approach to healing considered in this section is for the conscious mind of the healer to impress telepathically the subconscious mind of the patient. The most effective way to influence the subconscious mind is to send a symbolic picture. There are three types of symbolic pictures that are appropriate for physical healing work, and each will be discussed separately.

In the first type of picture, *the healer visualizes the patient as being healthy and whole but without specifically visualizing his inner organs.* For instance, the patient might be pictured as performing a strenuous physical exercise that could only be accomplished if he were healthy. This first method does not require the healer to have any knowledge about physiology or even about the patient's illness.[23]

In the second type of picture, *the healer visualizes the diseased organs of the patient's body as being healthy.* Now the healer should have some knowledge of physiology in order to know which organs are associated with the patient's illness and how these organs would appear in a healthy state. Yogi Ramacharaka gives the following instructions for this approach:

> In giving mental healing treatments, the mind of the healer must be able to picture the desired conditions in the patient—that is to mentally *see* the patient as healed, and the parts, organs and cells functioning normally. In short, in the degree that the healer is able to mentally visualize the normal conditions, so will be the degree of success in mental healing. . . . So far as transmitting the thought is concerned, that requires no strenuous effort on the part of

the healer. The main difficulty lies in the ability to form the mental image, just described—that once formed the thought is easily transmitted by *merely thinking of it as occurring.*[24]

The first two types of imagery could be thought of as being static methods because the healer envisions only the desired healthy state. In the third type, *the healer visualizes the internal operations that should be performed in order for the patient to go from his present unhealthy state to the desired healthy state,* and thus it is a dynamic approach. This third type could be considered as a mental analogue of a physical operation, and the healer now needs to have considerable medical knowledge, just as he would for a physical operation. Although this third type of imagery has the potential of producing a more rapid recovery than the first two types, the possibility of making a mistake and harming the patient is also greater, so the healer should proceed with great care. Bibb and Weed recommend this third method, and they emphasize that the transmitted instructions need be only in symbolic terms:

> The pictures or scenarios you send are not offered in the expectation they will be slavishly followed. The inner mind of the subject has its own methods for handling the situation once it gets a general idea of what must be done to effect a cure. The simplest pictures are best. If a muscle is torn, tie it together. If a subject's lungs are filled with mucus, use a vacuum cleaner. If there is a growth to be removed, pluck it out with your fingers. Never, never visualize the use of a knife: there should be no cutting. You are to heal tissues, not destroy them. If a tooth is loose, take it out with your fingers mentally, clean it thoroughly and return it after first packing the cavity with glue (mental, of course).[25]

For each of the three foregoing approaches, the effort is to convey visualized pictures to the patient's subconscious mind. It also may be desirable to convey mental statements, sometimes called decrees, affirming that the healing will take place. The images and statements begin with the healer's mental body and throat chakra, are transmitted from his solar plexus chakra, are registered by the patient's solar plexus chakra, and finally reach the patient's subconscious mind.[26]

For successful transmission, the solar plexus is the only chakra that needs to be developed for either healer or patient, which means that this procedure is a potentially useful method for physical healing. The healer also must have skill in visualization, and the patient must be willing to receive the telepathic help. In other words, the patient must be open on an emotional level to the healer's influence, thus permitting the patient's subconscious mind to respond to the healer's guidance.

Although the patient need not be hypnotized during the telepathic treatment, there is a similarity to hypnotherapy because the healer proceeds by influencing the patient's subconscious mind. But this approach is superior to hypnotherapy from a spiritual perspective because the patient need not sacrifice his free choice. At any moment the patient can choose to stop receiving the telepathic treatment, simply by closing his subconscious mind to the healer's influence.

Telepathic healing, when successful, produces deeper results than does treatment with prana, because an aspect of the subconscious mind is deeper than the etheric body. When telepathic and pranic healing are combined, which sometimes occurs, it is recommended that the telepathic work be done first in order to help the patient become properly receptive to the pranic energy. Nevertheless, the results from this combined effort may be only temporary if the underlying cause of the physical illness is an inner emotional or mental conflict that has not yet been resolved.

Chapter 6

Radiatory Healing

This chapter will examine healing by the radiation of monadic qualities to the patient. The first step is for the healer to experience the monadic qualities within himself, which means to experience inner alignment, mental clarity, compassion, and inner peace; then he is able to radiate those qualities merely by intending to do so. The purpose of this chapter is to explain how this type of healing actually occurs, in terms of the chakras and other aspects of a person's inner constitution. The causal body will be considered first because of its key role in transmitting qualities from higher dimensions. But it should be remembered throughout this discussion that the actual practice of radiatory healing is relatively simple and that the technical explanation is included only for describing this process.

Egoic Lotus

Chapter 1 characterized the causal body as being the vehicle of abstract thought, storehouse for the wisdom gained from all experiences, and conveyer of qualities from higher dimensions. Two different pictorial descriptions of the causal body have been given:

Egoic lotus. Bailey conceives of the causal body in the form of a twelve-petaled lotus, called the egoic lotus, which consists of nine outer petals surrounding three inner petals. For an undeveloped person, this lotus is described as having the appearance of an unopened bud; but during the course of evolution, these petals slowly unfold as an individual gains wisdom from his experiences.[1]

Concentric shells of color. Leadbeater published a series of pictures, presumably based on his own paranormal observations, illustrating the evolution of the causal body—beginning with that of a savage, then average man, developed man, and finally "arhat." Leadbeater says that the causal body of a savage "resembles the soap-bubble in being almost empty in appearance." But in an arhat the colors "are arranged in great concentric shells, yet penetrated everywhere by radiations of living light always pouring forth from him as a center."[2]

Bailey's description is clearly a symbolic attempt to convey the nature of the causal body, and she cautions that "the student must be careful not to materialise his concept too much."[3] On the other hand, Leadbeater's description is based on paranormal observations as interpreted by his physical brain. Thus, these descriptions are not really in conflict but instead serve different purposes. Bailey's symbology is employed in the following discussion.

Chapter 1 described the causal body as a "bridge" that enables the personality to consciously receive spiritual qualities from the monad. Evolving the causal body is equivalent to unfolding the petals of the egoic lotus, which in turn is equivalent to a person abstracting wisdom from his experiences. The spiritual qualities represented by the monad are only latent in an unevolved person because he is not aware of them. However, the unfoldment of the petals of the egoic lotus symbolizes his awakening to the presence of these inner qualities. This awakening is the bridge that enables these spiritual qualities to be expressed outwardly, resulting in a transmission of energy from the monad to the personality vehicles.

Bailey has divided the nine outer petals of the egoic lotus into three categories, each consisting of three petals:

1. *The sacrifice petals,* which transmit energy from the spiritual will;

2. *The love petals,* which transmit energy from the spiritual love; and

3. *The knowledge petals,* which transmit energy from the spiritual mind.

She also has given the meaning of each category of petals, and of each petal within each category, in terms of the specific learning needed for unfoldment.[4]

Lines of Transmission

In the practice of radiatory healing, Bailey states that the healer must first energize his personality vehicles with "soul energy" received from his egoic lotus, and that he then can use his "aura" for transmitting this energy to the patient.[5] She defines the aura as being composed of the outgoing vibratory effect of the etheric chakras, and that these vibrations can embody etheric, emotional, and mental energies.[6] Thus, the qualities the healer receives from his egoic lotus can be transformed by his etheric chakras into vibratory waves that are transmitted via the planetary etheric body to the patient. Because this radiation occurs at the etheric level, this chapter will use the word "chakra" to refer only to an etheric force center, and not to a center belonging to a higher vehicle. As discussed in earlier chapters, the planetary etheric body is also used as the medium for both pranic and telepathic work.

The lines of transmission in radiatory healing are outlined in Table 11 on page 82. There is a line originating from each of the three aspects of the monad (which is the healer's essential spiritual nature), transmitted through the spiritual triad (which is the reflection of that nature in the field of manifestation), through the egoic lotus (which is his conscious awareness of his inner qualities), through the personality vehicles (which is where these inner qualities are expressed), through the healer's chakras (which radiate the energies), and then out to the patient. Although each energy stream must pass through all three personality vehicles (mental, emotional, and etheric) before reaching the etheric chakras, Table 11 lists only one of these vehicles for each stream. The reason is that each stream especially qualifies or affects the personality body listed. In particular, the spiritual will is reflected in the higher aspect of the etheric body, the spiritual love is reflected in the emotional body, and the spiritual mind is reflected in the mental body.[7]

Next, each line of transmission is considered separately. The will quality from the healer's monad is transmitted through his spiritual will, sacrifice petals, etheric body, and crown chakra before being radiated from his brow chakra. The patient registers these auric emanations with his crown chakra; they then aid him in becoming aligned with his own spiritual will.[8] The love-wisdom quality from the healer's monad is transmitted through his spiritual love, love petals, and emotional body before being radiated from both his heart and solar plexus chakras. The

Table 11. Lines of Transmission in Radiatory Healing*

Radiation of Will	Radiation of Love-Wisdom	Radiation of Active Intelligence
Monad: will aspect	Monad: love-wisdom aspect	Monad: active intelligence aspect
Spiritual will (atmic permanent atom)	Spiritual love (buddhic permanent atom)	Spiritual mind (mental permanent atom)
Sacrifice petals of egoic lotus	Love petals of egoic lotus	Knowledge petals of egoic lotus
Etheric body in its higher aspect	Emotional body	Mental body, or lower concrete mind
Crown and brow chakras of healer	Heart and solar plexus chakras of healer	Throat chakra of healer
Crown chakra of patient	Heart and solar plexus chakras of patient	Throat chakra of patient
Aids the patient in becoming aligned with his own spiritual will	Aids the patient in awakening a sense of compassion and calming his emotions	Aids the patient in strengthening and clarifying his mind

*The material in this table has been adapted from Alice Bailey's *A Treatise on Cosmic Fire*, page 817.

patient registers the heart emanations with his heart chakra, and these aid in stimulating a sense of compassion.[9] He registers the solar plexus emanations with his solar plexus chakra; they aid in calming his emotions.[10] The active intelligence quality from the healer's monad is transmitted through his spiritual mind, knowledge petals, and mental body before being radiated from his throat chakra. The patient registers these auric emanations with his throat chakra. They aid in strengthening and clarifying his mind.[11]

Telepathy and radiatory healing are similar but with the following difference: As discussed in Chapter 5, the telepathic worker attempts to transmit a definite symbol, idea, or message to a recipient, and this message may have intuitional, mental, and emotional aspects; the radiatory healer attempts to transmit his own inner experience of alignment, mental clarity, compassion, and peace, which in turn are the results of having received the corresponding qualities from his spiritual triad. The telepathic worker is occupied mainly with the clarity of his message, whereas the radiatory healer is occupied mainly with abiding in the highest state of consciousness that he can experience. The chakra relationships for telepathy in Table 10 are consistent with those given for radiation in Table 11.

Etheric Radiation

We have just considered radiatory healing from a vertical perspective, that is, the transformation of force from one plane to another. In contrast, we will now emphasize a horizontal perspective, meaning the radiation of force from healer to patient. As discussed earlier, the energies actually radiated to the patient take the form of wavelike vibrations of etheric substance, but these vibrations embody monadic qualities. This section will refer to these radiations as "monadic energies," even though they are etheric in substance, and will use the terms *will, love-wisdom,* and *active intelligence* to designate the three types of monadic energies.

Both healer and patient should fulfill certain conditions for radiatory healing to be successful. The healer should be able first to experience the monadic qualities within himself and then be able to radiate the corresponding vibrations. This process requires that certain of his etheric chakras be developed. In particular, the healer needs to have his basic chakra active and brow chakra developed to radiate the will energy from his brow chakra;[12] his heart chakra should be developed to radiate the love-wisdom energy from that chakra;[13] his throat chakra should be active to radiate the active intelligence energy from that chakra; and his heart chakra should be active and solar plexus chakra developed to radiate the love-wisdom energy from his solar plexus chakra.

For proper registration, the patient should have some of his chakras active plus a willingness to register the radiated energies—the word *willingness* is used because his experience is subject to his own free choice. In particular, if the patient is "highly developed," then his crown chakra would be sufficiently active to register the will energy, and his heart chakra would be sufficiently active to register the love-wisdom energy. If he is "an ordinary and average advanced person," then his throat chakra would be sufficiently active to register the active intelligence energy. But even if the patient is "quite undeveloped and relatively a low grade human being," then his solar plexus chakra would still be sufficiently active to register the love-wisdom energy.[14]

A chakra can be thought of as being an oscillator with a particular natural frequency. An *oscillator* can be described as any object that moves in a regular periodic manner, such as a violin string or a pendulum. Two oscillators having the same natural frequency can develop *sympathetic resonance,* which means that the vibrations of one oscillator can reinforce those of the other. For example, if a string in one violin is played while a second violin lies on a table, then the corresponding string in that second violin will begin to vibrate. In this case, vibratory waves are passed through the air from one violin to the other. In the same way, if several pendulum clocks are hung on the same wall, so that the pendulums are of the same length but are out of phase, after a while all clocks will be in phase. Here, vibratory waves are passed through the wall from one clock to another.[15]

Consequently, radiatory healing can be understood as a process of establishing sympathetic resonance between corresponding chakras in healer and patient. In this case, vibratory waves are transferred over the etheric subplanes, thereby enabling the patient's chakras to become "synchronized" with those of the healer.[16]

Although this section has focused on radiatory work in terms of the chakras, other authors have described this type of activity in other terms. For example, Leadbeater describes it as projecting harmony:

> The operator endeavors to bring himself into a condition of intense harmony and peace and devotion, and then to project this influence upon the patient, or to enfold him in it. The practitioner...does not care to know what is the matter with the patient; the nature of the disease is of no importance to him; in any case it must be discord, and he can cure it by establishing harmony once more.[17]

Goldsmith describes it as conveying the experience of inner peace: "We have only to retire into our own sanctuary and find this peace, and when it has been found, our household and all those who are attuned to us take on a measure of that same peace in proportion to their receptivity."[18] However, A Course in Miracles does seem to refer to the heart chakra in the following passage: "The peace of God is shining in you now, and from your heart extends around the world. It pauses to caress each living thing, and leaves a blessing with it that remains forever and forever.... It brings renewal to all tired hearts, and lights all vision as it passes by."[19]

As indicated by these quotations, some presentations of radiatory healing do not mention the chakras. The explanation is that a person's intention automatically controls the activity of his chakras, which generally operate below the threshold of consciousness. Thus, a practitioner can transmit various qualities to a patient without understanding which centers send or receive the corresponding vibrations. After first experiencing those qualities within himself, a healer can radiate them merely by intending to do so, which causes the requisite activity of his chakras to occur automatically. The fundamental requirement for a healer is that there be sufficient evolution in his causal body, thus enabling him to express "right living, high thinking and loving activity," which in turn result in the required development of his chakras. But technical knowledge about the chakras is definitely not necessary.[20]

Practical Instructions

It is possible to improve the effectiveness of radiatory healing; the following suggestions are based on the principle that "energy follows thought," which means that the healer is able to direct the movement of his etheric energies mentally. This section will also show how technical knowledge regarding the chakras can be helpful.

If the healer perceives that a particular type of monadic energy is especially therapeutic for the patient, then he can choose to stimulate mentally his own corresponding chakra to increase the amplitude of its radiation. As an analogy, such dense physical organs as the heart and stomach generally function automatically below the threshold of consciousness, but it has been demonstrated in biofeedback research that a person can exercise volitional control over these seemingly involuntary organs.[21] Similarly, the etheric chakras generally function automatically below the threshold of consciousness, but the healer also can choose to stimulate mentally the radiatory activity of any selected chakra.[22]

During contact healing, there are additional ways to improve the effectiveness of the work. In the case of the love-wisdom or active intelligence radiation, it is suggested that the patient lie on his side, with the healer standing behind the patient. Because the spinal chakras are located outside and behind the dense physical body, this arrangement facilitates the entry of the healer's radiation into the patient's receiving chakra or chakras.[23] The healer may wish to use the minor chakras in his hands to focus the love-wisdom radiation directly at the patient's solar plexus chakra.[24] Figure 2 on page 19 illustrates the approximate location for this chakra, and the hands should be placed about three inches behind the patient's dense spine. In the case of the will radiation, it is suggested that the patient be lying down with the healer standing at the patient's head. This arrangement facilitates the flow of energy from the healer's brow to the patient's crown chakra.[25] The healer also may wish to use his hand chakras to focus the will radiation at the patient's crown chakra, with his hands held just above the top of the patient's head but without actually touching him.[26]

Absent healing refers to a practitioner sending energy to a patient who is at a distance away. Pranic, telepathic, and monadic energies all can be sent as part of absent healing. The first step is for the healer to vitalize an etheric cord linking his etheric body with the patient's, which is done by the healer sending the quality of positive regard via his solar plexus emanations; and the second step is for him to send one or more of the healing energies. For an average healer, the intensity of influence diminishes as the distance increases, just as radio wave intensity depends on distance from the transmitter. On the other hand, the intensity of absent healing can be amplified through group activity in which several workers combine their energies. It is important that the patient be able to register the transmitted energies. To improve this registration, some healers request that their patients become deliberately receptive to the healing influences at specific times during the day.

In Chapter 4 the role of a "higher intelligence" in pranic healing was discussed. This intelligence also can participate in radiatory healing, provided the healer has both earned and invoked such assistance. Bailey describes how a discarnate "Master" can enhance the healer's radiatory activity by directing vibratory energy along three lines: by radiating energy from the atmic plane—which affects the healer's spiritual will, then his sacrifice petals, etheric vehicle, crown center, and brow center; radiating energy from the buddhic plane—which affects the healer's spiritual love, then his love petals, emotional body, heart center, and solar plexus center; and radiating energy from the higher levels of the mental plane—which affects the healer's spiritual mind, then his knowledge petals, mental body, and finally throat center.[27] Thus, by means of invocation, the healer is able to increase significantly the potency of his radiation.

Chapter 7

Conclusions

Earlier chapters have described in some detail theories relating the chakras, states of consciousness, and the following types of healing with subtle energies: *pranic healing,* which can stimulate the vitality within the patient's physical body; *telepathic healing,* which can affect the patient's mental attitudes and subconscious mind; and *radiatory healing,* which can aid the patient in calming his emotions, stimulating compassion, strengthening his mind, and bringing him into alignment. Table 12 on page 90 summarizes the relationships between the chakras and these modes of healing.

Chapters 4, 5, and 6 indicated that a practitioner could accomplish pranic, telepathic, and radiatory healing without having any knowledge of the locations and functions of the chakras. What then is the value of relating the chakras to healing?

The chakras provide a coherent theory of the healing process. Although esoteric healing is very ancient, it is not understood at all by modern science. Thus, there is some value in having a theory that explains how healing with subtle energies may work, in terms of subtle force centers and the inner human constitution. The relationships summarized in Table 12 are only speculative from the point of view of modern science, as there is little scientific evidence currently available that supports them. However, other types of supportive evidence are available, such as experiences of healers, paranormal investigations, and the tradition of Hindu yoga.

Table 12. Relationship Between Etheric Chakras and Modes of Healing

Mode of Healing	Chakra Used in Transmission	Chakra Used in Reception	Purpose
Pranic			
Brow distribution	Brow	Any center	To vitalize any of the patient's organs
Solar plexus distribution	Solar plexus	Solar plexus	To vitalize any organ associated with the solar plexus chakra
Splenic distribution	Splenic	Sacral	To vitalize any organ associated with the sacral chakra
Telepathic			
Causal body to causal body	Crown, brow	Crown	To transmit an intuitive understanding of an idea that may affect the patient's mental attitude
Mental body to mental body	Throat, solar plexus	Throat, solar plexus	To transmit a concrete thought that may affect the patient's mental attitude
Mental body to subconscious	Throat, solar plexus	Solar plexus	To transmit instructions to the patient's subconscious mind on how to cure physical illness
Radiatory			
Will	Crown, brow	Crown	To bring the patient into alignment with his own spiritual will
Active intelligence	Throat	Throat	To strengthen and clarify the patient's mind
Love-wisdom	Heart, solar plexus	Heart, solar plexus	To awaken a sense of compassion in the patient and calm his emotions

The chakras provide a basis for a student to learn the art of healing. For example, a student could begin by visualizing the flow of each energy from its source, through his own chakras, and then out to the patient, thereby taking advantage of the law that "energy follows thought." But practice is required for an effective healing ability.

The chakras determine the capacity of the healer to heal. The healer is able to send energy from only those centers within his etheric body that are developed; this will determine the types of pranic, telepathic, and monadic energies that can be conveyed. Ideally, he should make an honest appraisal of his own point of evolution. If the healer lacks the capacity to send the specific energies needed by a particular patient, then he should recognize that fact and refuse to waste the patient's time.

The chakras determine the capacity of the patient to respond to healing. The patient's intention controls the activity of his chakras. Thus, in any mode of esoteric healing, effective results generally require that the patient request this assistance, trust the healer, and truly wish to be healed, in order for the patient's chakras to be receptive to the healer's influence. The patient is able to respond to treatment with prana irrespective of his chakra development, but his chakras must be sufficiently active in order to register telepathic impressions and monadic energies. For example, it was stated in Chapter 5 that the healer could transmit an intuitive understanding of an idea that may affect the patient's mental attitude, but this would be successful only if the patient were fairly evolved and had an active crown chakra.

The chakras can improve the effectiveness of the healing work. Although technical knowledge of the chakras is not necessary for accomplishing any mode of esoteric healing, such knowledge can improve the effectiveness of the work. For example, it was discussed in Chapter 6 how this knowledge could enable the practitioner to use his hands for focusing and distributing love-wisdom emanations directly at a patient's chakra, thereby increasing the effective intensity of the radiation.

The chakras explain some of the experiences that both healer and patient undergo. Because the etheric body is below the threshold of consciousness, a person generally is not aware of the energy flows within his system but only recognizes a general sense of vitality or depletion. Nevertheless, the healer can experience a number of sensations that are explained by chakra relationships. For example, it was stated in Chapter 4 that the pranic healer may experience pressure in his head area, tingling in his hands, and a spontaneous need to breathe rhythmically. As far as the patient is concerned, the associations between chakras and endocrine glands indicate one way that prana affects the dense physical body.

The chakras may aid the patient in healing himself. The patient often can heal himself merely by having an objective attitude toward his illness and any underlying difficulty. This objective attitude can be achieved through meditation. Chapter 3 described how knowledge of the chakras may help the person to practice meditation by helping him to understand the nature of his higher states of consciousness.

As was said earlier, there is currently little scientific evidence that supports the theories presented in the preceding chapters. Although chakras and subtle forms of healing may seem to be intrinsically difficult to study scientifically, there is actually great potential for laboratory research in this area, and in fact several scientific studies already have been performed. For instance, Chapter 2 referred to experimental research concerning physiological effects of chakra development. In another investigation, physiological changes have been measured in subjects receiving absent healing.[1] The effects of healing energy also have been studied on mice,[2] enzyme growth,[3] and water.[4] However, much more research is needed.

The five appendices that follow give interpretations, in terms of the chakras, of previously published symbolic formulas that heretofore have never been fully explained. Appendix I summarizes techniques for healing others; Appendix II outlines a systematic approach to self-healing; Appendix III depicts the stages of chakra evolution; Appendix IV describes the experiences of chakra development; and Appendix V gives instructions for attaining higher consciousness.

Formulas for Healing Others

The first three appendices will interpret three sets of symbolic formulas that were originally published by Alice A. Bailey; however, the interpretations that follow are solely the responsibility of this writer and may not be what Bailey originally intended.

The first set of symbolic formulas is concerned with healing others. Bailey published these formulas without explaining them but anticipated that they would eventually be understood because she predicted that "some disciple in the early part of next century will take these techniques or magical statements, relating to the healing work, and interpret them and elucidate them."[1] However, she gave an important clue by saying that these formulas "are susceptible of three significances, the lowest of which the modern student may succeed in interpreting for himself if he reflects adequately and lives spiritually."[2] As will be shown in this appendix, each symbolic formula corresponds to a ray quality, a technique of esoteric healing, and a technique of exoteric healing. The interpretation in terms of esoteric healing will be described first.

First Formula

Let the dynamic force which rules the hearts of all within Shamballa come to my aid, for I am worthy of that aid. Let it descend unto the third, pass to the fifth and focus on the seventh. These words mean not what doth at sight appear. The third, the fifth, the seventh lie within the first and come from out the Central Sun of spiritual livingness. The highest then awakens within the one who knows and within the one who must be healed and thus the two are one. This is mystery deep. The blending of the healing force effects the work desired; it may bring death, that great release, and re-establish thus the fifth, the third, the first, but not the seventh. [3]

This first formula refers to the etheric radiation of the monadic will energy. Because "the third, the fifth, the seventh lie within the first," the initial enumeration refers to the seven planes that interpenetrate. In esoteric literature, the word *Shamballa* is associated with the monadic will quality. As outlined in Table 11, the will quality must descend through the spiritual will (on the "third" or atmic plane), through the egoic lotus or causal body (on the "fifth" or mental plane), before reaching the etheric body (on the "seventh" or physical plane). The "highest" etheric chakra is the crown, which is then used by the healer when radiating the will energy and by the patient when registering that energy. As a result, both healer and patient can be motivated by the same dynamic force ("the two are one").

However, the enumeration in the formula's last sentence refers to the major chakras, where the "first" is the crown and the "seventh" is the basic. If the patient is mentally polarized and spiritually oriented, then during death the energies of his etheric body can become focused in his crown chakra, which would enable him to die with full consciousness. In this case, the withdrawing energies will pass up the spine, sequentially stimulating the major chakras ("the fifth, the third, the first, but not the seventh"), before the consciousness stream is finally released from the crown chakra.

Second Formula

Let the healing energy descend, carrying its dual lines of life and its magnetic force. Let that magnetic living force withdraw and supplement that which is present in the seventh, opposing four and six to three and seven, but dealing not with five. The circular, inclusive vortex—descending to the point—disturbs, removes and then supplies and thus the work is done.

The heart revolves; two hearts revolve as one; the twelve within the vehicle, the twelve within the head and the twelve upon the plane of soul endeavour, cooperate as one and thus the work is done. Two energies achieve this consummation and the three whose number is a twelve respond to the greater twelve. The life is known and the years prolonged.[4]

Chapter 4 stated that prana is qualified by the etheric energies acting within the healer's etheric body. This second formula refers to transmitting prana that has been qualified by the love-wisdom energy, where this prana is specialized for either the heart, solar plexus, sacral, or basic chakra. In the first paragraph of the quotation from Bailey above, the "dual lines of life" refer to both pranic and life stream energies, and "magnetic force" refers to the love-wisdom energy qualifying that prana. The love-wisdom energy is registered by the heart chakra, which can control the solar plexus chakra, which in turn can influence the lower chakras.

The patient's illness may be the result of an inner conflict between his higher nature (or spiritual triad) and lower nature (or personality). The enumeration in the first paragraph of the quotation from Bailey refers to the seven planes. The spiritual love is on the fourth (or buddhic) plane and may be in opposition to emotional reactions in the emotional body on the sixth (or emotional) plane. The spiritual will is on the third (or atmic) plane and may be in opposition to vital reactions in the etheric body on the seventh (or physical) plane. The spiritual mind is on the fifth (or mental) plane and may be in opposition to mental reactions in the mental body also on the fifth plane. The formula states that this type of healing is able to alleviate the etheric effects ("supplement that which is present in the seventh") due to some of these conflicts: between the spiritual love and emotional reactions ("opposing four and six"), between the spiritual will and vital reactions ("three and seven"), but not between the spiritual mind and mental reactions ("but dealing not with five"). Alleviating the latter would require prana specialized for the throat chakra.

A chakra is sometimes symbolized as a lotus consisting of several petals, and the number of petals for each lotus is shown in Figure 3 (see page 56). According to this perspective, the crown chakra is symbolized as having an inner circle of twelve petals, surrounded by an outer circle of nine hundred and sixty petals. The inner circle of twelve petals is sometimes called the "heart within the head." The brow chakra is symbolized as being divided into two primary petals, each of which is further subdivided into forty-eight smaller petals, so that there are ninety-six petals altogether. The heart chakra is symbolized as having twelve petals. As discussed in Chapter 6, the egoic lotus on the mental plane also has twelve petals. For the purpose of understanding this formula, it is important to note that all these numbers are multiples of twelve.

The second paragraph indicates that the work of pranic healing requires the cooperation of the crown, brow, and heart chakras ("the three whose number is a twelve"), the consciousness and life streams ("the two energies"), and the egoic lotus ("the twelve upon the plane of soul endeavor" or "the greater twelve"). The healer's consciousness stream, which connects his crown chakra with his egoic lotus, can ensure that the distributed prana is qualified by only the love-wisdom energy received by the heart chakra and not by any negative feelings. The healer's life stream, which connects his heart chakra with his egoic lotus, can control the circulation of prana. And the healer's brow chakra can be used to distribute specialized prana to any of the patient's centers.

Third Formula

The healer stands and weaves. He gathers from the three, the five, the seven that which is needed for the heart of life. He brings the energies together and makes them serve the third; he thus creates a vortex into which the one distressed must descend and with him goes the healer. And yet they both remain in peace and calm. Thus must the angel of the Lord descend into the pool and bring the healing life.[5]

This third formula refers to the etheric radiation of the active intelligence energy. The enumeration in this paragraph may be confusing, because it mixes several types of symbols. Whereas "the three" refers to the active intelligence quality, which is considered to be the third aspect of the monad, "the five" and "the seven" refer to the fifth and seventh planes, and "the third" refers to the third or throat chakra. As outlined in Table 11 on page 82, the active intelligence quality must pass through the spiritual mind, egoic lotus, and mental body, which are all on the fifth or mental plane, before reaching the etheric chakras on the seventh or physical plane. The "third" or throat chakra is then used by the healer when radiating the active intelligence energy and by the patient when registering that energy. It is the task of the mental body ("the angel of the Lord") to control the emotional body ("the pool"). The active intelligence radiation strengthens and clarifies the patient's concrete thinking, thereby helping him to bring "peace and calm" to his emotions and activate his heart chakra ("heart of life").

Fourth Formula

The healer knows the place where dissonance is found. He also knows the power of sound and the sound which must be heard. Knowing the note to which the fourth great group reacts and linking it to the great Creative Nine, he sounds the note which brings release, the note which will bring absorption into one. He educates the listening ear of him who must be healed; he likewise trains the listening ear of him who must go forth. He knows the manner of the sound which brings the healing touch; and also that which says: Depart. And thus the work is done.[6]

This fourth formula refers to the etheric radiation of the love-wisdom energy from the heart chakra. As outlined in Table 11, the love-wisdom quality ("power of sound") must pass through the spiritual love ("sound which must be heard"), nine outer petals of the egoic lotus ("great Creative Nine"), emotional body ("knowing the note"), before the healer radiates this energy ("sounds the note") from his fourth or heart chakra ("fourth great group"). The patient registers the love-wisdom energy with his heart chakra ("listening ear"), which enables him to experience compassion or a sense of oneness with others ("absorption into one").

Fifth Formula

That which has been given must be used; that which emerges from within the given mode will find its place within the healer's plan. That which is hidden must be seen and from the three, great knowledge will emerge. For these the healer seeks. To these the healer adds the two which are as one, and so the fifth must play its part and the five must play its part and the five must function as if one. The energies descend, pass through and disappear, leaving the one who could respond with karma yet to dissipate and taking with them him who may not thus respond and so must likewise disappear.[7]

This fifth formula refers to transmitting prana that has been qualified by the active intelligence energy, where this prana is specialized for the throat chakra. As outlined in Table 11, the active intelligence quality ("that which has been given") must pass through the spiritual mind ("that which emerges from within the given mode"), egoic lotus ("that which is hidden"), and mental body ("great knowledge"), before emerging from the third or throat chakra ("the three"). To this the healer adds the pranic and life stream energies ("the two which are as one") by utilizing the following "five" chakras: splenic, heart, throat, brow, and crown. The healer's splenic chakra is used to absorb prana from the atmosphere. The life stream anchored in his heart chakra is used to control the circulation of prana. Specialized prana is raised to the healer's throat chakra where it is qualified by the active intelligence energy received from the spiritual mind, egoic lotus, and mental body, which are all on the "fifth" or mental plane. The qualified throat prana is then raised to the healer's brow center for distribution to the patient. And the healer's crown chakra is used to maintain self-awareness, thus ensuring that the prana is not qualified by negative thought patterns.

Sixth Formula

Cleaving the waters, let the power descend, the healer cries. He minds not how the waters may respond; they oft bring stormy waves and dire and dreadful happenings. The end is good. The trouble will be ended when the storm subsides and energy has fulfilled its charted destiny. Straight to the heart the power is forced to penetrate, and into every channel, nadi, nerve and spleen the power must seek a passage and a way and thus confront the enemy who has effected entrance and settled down to live. Ejection— ruthless, sudden and complete—is undertaken by the one who sees naught else but perfect functioning and brooks no interference. This perfect functioning opens thus the door to life eternal or to life on earth for yet a little while.[8]

This sixth formula refers to radiating the love-wisdom energy from the solar plexus chakra. The healer's first steps are to eliminate his own negative feelings ("cleaving the waters") and to experience the love-wisdom quality ("let the power descend"). His intent is to replace the patient's emotional turmoil ("stormy waves and dire and dreadful happenings") with inner peace ("the end is good"). The healer's approach is to radiate the love-wisdom energy to the patient's solar plexus chakra ("the heart"), which will then affect the latter's sympathetic nervous system ("every channel, nadi, nerve and spleen"). The patient's anxiety ("the enemy") can be completely ended, provided that the healer maintains his own inner peace during this process ("sees naught else but perfect functioning and brooks no interference").

Seventh Formula

Energy and force must meet each other and thus the work is done. Colour and sound in ordered sequence must meet and blend and thus the work of magic can proceed. Substance and spirit must evoke each other and, passing through the centre of the one who seeks to aid, produce the new and good. The healer energises thus with life the failing life, driving it forth or anchoring it yet more deeply in the place of destiny. All seven must be used and through the seven there must pass the energies the need requires, creating the new man who has for ever been and will for ever be, and either here or there.[9]

This seventh and final formula refers to transmitting prana that has been qualified by the will energy, where this prana is specialized for either the crown or brow chakra. The formula states that "all seven must be used," meaning that the healer must activate all seven of his major chakras; and that "through the seven there must pass the energies the need requires," meaning that the kundalini energy from the basic chakra must pass through the seven major chakras until it reaches the crown chakra, in order for the latter to clearly register the will energy. The healer uses his life stream ("spirit") to evoke additional prana ("substance") from the atmosphere. After the prana is specialized for each major chakra ("in ordered sequence"), the will energy ("sound") can blend with and qualify the specialized crown or brow prana ("color"). The work is done when the healer's qualified prana ("energy") meets the patient's etheric condition ("force").

Other Interpretations

The preceding portion of this appendix discussed how each formula can be interpreted as giving a technique of esoteric healing: the first formula corresponds to radiating the will energy; the second, to transmitting prana qualified by the love-wisdom energy; the third, to radiating the active intelligence energy; the fourth, to radiating the love-wisdom energy from the heart chakra; the fifth, to transmitting prana qualified by the active intelligence energy; the sixth, to radiating the love-wisdom energy from the solar plexus chakra; and the seventh, to transmitting prana qualified by the will energy.

However, the symbols used in each formula also can be interpreted as giving a technique of exoteric healing: the first formula corresponds to healing by being an inspiring example; the second, to intuitive counseling; the third, to improving the patient's environment; the fourth, to using color and sound; the fifth, to education; the sixth, to medicine; and the seventh, to using crystals. The detailed analysis of the formulas in terms of these exoteric methods will be left to the reader.

In esoteric philosophy a "ray" is defined as a particular *quality* of energy; therefore, the same ray can be expressed by several energies having different *form* aspects. It is said that there are seven different rays or qualities of energy, and a definite name has been given to each ray.[10] Each of the preceding formulas can be associated with one of the seven rays, in the sense that the corresponding esoteric or exoteric healing technique expresses the specific quality represented by that ray. The first formula can be interpreted as corresponding to the ray of will; the second, to the ray of love-wisdom; the third, to the ray of active intelligence; the fourth, to the ray of harmony; the fifth, to the ray of concrete knowledge; the sixth, to the ray of devotion; and the seventh, to the ray of ceremonial magic.

In summary, each symbolic formula can be associated with a ray, a technique of esoteric healing, and a technique of exoteric healing. One can think of each ray as representing a specific healing quality, the associated esoteric technique as embodying that quality on an etheric level, and the associated exoteric technique as embodying that same quality on a dense physical level. In this way the seven symbolic formulas help to describe a comprehensive philosophy of healing.

Appendix II

Rules for Self-Healing

Magic can be defined as the ability to produce material things from the unseen universe. Alice A. Bailey has published fifteen "rules for magic" that purport to describe the process of magic. Unfortunately, the terminology in these rules was deliberately chosen to be "in the nature of a blind, which ever carries revelation to those who have the clue, but tends to perplex and to bewilder the student who as yet is unready for the truth."[1] However, Bailey did say that these rules could be interpreted on several levels, including that of the intelligent man, aspirant, disciple, and initiate.[2]

Although other meanings could be given to these rules, they will be interpreted here as providing a systematic approach to self-healing. But if the reader wishes to apply these rules to cure a serious illness, then it is recommended that he work closely with a qualified physician. Each of the following sections consists of three parts: the rule itself, the meaning of its symbols, and its interpretation in terms of self-healing.

First Rule

The Solar Angel collects himself, scatters not his force, but in meditation deep communicates with his reflection.[3]

In this first rule, the "Solar Angel" refers to the causal body (or soul), "communicates" refers to transmitting intuitive understanding, and "reflection" refers to the personality.

Because the causal body is always in a meditative state, it is aligned and focused, and thus can transmit intuitive understanding to the personality.

Second Rule

When the shadow hath responded, in meditation deep the work proceedeth. The lower light is thrown upward; the greater light illuminates the three, and the work of the four proceedeth. [4]

The "shadow" refers to the personality, "lower light" to consciousness, "greater light" to intuitive understanding, "three" to the personality consisting of the mental, emotional, and physical bodies, and "four" to the aligned causal body and personality.

When the patient's personality responds by also attaining a meditative state, then the effort of self-healing can proceed. Thus, the patient must elevate his consciousness, so that his personality becomes aligned, focused, and receptive. As a result, intuitive understanding can be received which illuminates his mental, emotional, and physical natures, thereby enabling his causal body and personality to work together in an integrated way.

Third Rule

The Energy circulates. The point of light, the product of the labours of the Four, waxeth and groweth. The myriads gather round its glowing warmth until its light recedes. Its fire grows dim. Then shall the second sound go forth. [5]

The "Energy circulates" refers to receiving an intuitive image of wholeness, "point of light" to the focused energy used for visualization, "Four" to the aligned causal, mental, emotional, and physical bodies, "myraids" to mental plane matter, and "second sound" to the visualized mental picture.

This rule has two parts. First, the patient receives (from his causal body) an intuitive image of wholeness: perhaps an image of himself as being vital and active, but without specifically revealing his inner organs; or an image of his diseased organs as being healthy; or an image of the internal operations needed for going from his present unhealthy state to his desired healthy state. Second, the patient endeavors to visualize a concrete mental picture corresponding to that intuitive image, which requires the focused energy of his aligned causal body and personality. As a result, mental matter is formed into a picture that is more concrete and tangible than the original intuitive image. This visualized picture will then go forth and acquire forms that are even more tangible.

Fourth Rule

Sound, light, vibration, and the form blend and merge, and thus the work is one. It proceedeth under the law, and naught can hinder now the work from going forward. The man breathes deeply. He concentrates his forces, and drives the thought-form from him.[6]

"Sound" refers to the intuitive image of wholeness; "light," to the focused energy used for visualization; "vibration," to the affected mental plane matter; "form," to the visualized mental picture; "breathes deeply," to inhalation; "concentrates his forces," to retention of breath; and "drives the thought-form from him," to exhalation.

When the intuitive image of wholeness is represented sufficiently well by the constructed mental picture, the step of visualization is completed. The work of manifesting that image in the dense physical body proceeds in an ordered way, and now the next step can be taken. To be successful, it is important that this effort be accompanied by organized rhythmic breathing. During inhalation, the patient achieves the meditative state as described in the second rule. During retention of breath, he receives an intuitive image and then visualizes a corresponding mental picture as described in the third rule. And during exhalation, he endeavors to add forms that are more tangible as described in the subsequent rules.

Fifth Rule

Three things engage the Solar Angel before the sheath created passes downward: the condition of the waters, the safety of the one who thus creates, and steady contemplation. Thus are the heart, the throat, and the eye, allied for triple service.[7]

The "Solar Angel" refers to the causal body; "sheath," to the intuitive image of wholeness; "condition of the waters," to the emotional feeling concerning the self-healing effort; "safety of the one who thus creates," to preserving the mental picture; "contemplation," to directing the process of etheric vitalization; and "heart, the throat, and the eye," to the heart, throat, and brow (or third eye) chakras.

The intuitive image of wholeness from the causal body must acquire three forms before this image can be manifested in the dense physical body: a mental picture must be created and preserved via the throat chakra; the proper emotional feeling must be established and maintained via the heart chakra; and the process of etheric vitalization and activity must be directed via the brow chakra.

Sixth Rule

The devas of the lower four feel the force when the eye opens; they are driven forth and lose their master.[8]

The "devas of the lower four" refer to the mental, emotional, etheric, and dense physical bodies. "Force" refers to intuitive understanding; "when the eye opens," to steady contemplation through the medium of the brow chakra; and "their master," to personality reactions.

The mental, emotional, etheric physical, and dense physical bodies represent four aspects of the personality, and each could be thought of as having its own individual life. These aspects may react to the discipline being imposed upon them by the preceding rule, which may then interfere with the self-healing process. When any of these personality aspects is steadily contemplated through the medium of the brow chakra, that aspect will feel the force of intuitive understanding. In this way the personality can be controlled, and undesirable reactions can be eliminated.

Seventh Rule

The dual forces on the plane whereon the vital power must be sought, are seen; the two paths face the Solar Angel; the poles vibrate. A choice confronts the one who meditates.[9]

The "plane whereon the vital power must be sought" refers to the emotional plane; "dual forces," to fear and desire; "two paths," to indulgence and inhibition; "Solar Angel," to the causal body; and "poles vibrate" refers to experiencing fear and desire.

To be successful, the patient must experience an emotional feeling that has the power to properly energize his self healing effort. However, he may instead experience two emotional reactions that can interfere with this process: fear that the healing may not occur; and desire for it to occur. If the patient tries to indulge or inhibit either of these feelings, then he may engender more of that same feeling. But if the patient, through meditation, can be guided by his causal body, then he can choose another way of controlling his emotional response.

Eighth Rule

The Agnisuryans respond to the sound. The waters ebb and flow. Let the magician guard himself from drowning at the point where land and water meet. The midway spot which is neither dry nor wet must provide the standing place where-

on his feet are set. When water, land and air meet there is
the place for magic to be wrought.[10]

The "Agnisuryans" refer to emotional plane matter. "Sound"
refers to the visualized mental picture; "waters," to the feelings being
experienced; "drowning," to being dominated by feelings; "land," to
the etheric body; "point where land and water meet," to the solar
plexus chakra; "midway spot which is neither dry nor wet," to the
mental body; "air," to intuitive understanding; and "place for magic to
be wrought," to the throat chakra.

Fear and desire are potential reactions of the emotional body to
the visualized mental picture, and either of these feelings could be an
interference. Thus, the patient must guard himself from being dominated by his solar plexus chakra, which is where the etheric body
registers emotional sensitivity. The mental body is the midway spot
between the emotional body and the causal body. When the patient is
focused in his mental body, he can be detached and objective towards
his feelings, and be guided by intuitive understanding. In this way, the
patient can identify the concrete thoughts and beliefs underlying any
feelings that would interfere with the self-healing effort, and then use
his throat chakra for changing those thoughts and beliefs, leading to
different feelings.

Ninth Rule

Condensation next ensues. The fire and waters meet, the
form swells and grows. Let the magician set his form upon
the proper path.[11]

"Condensation" refers to acquiring forms that are more tangible;
"fire," to etheric vitality, "waters," to emotional feelings; and "form,"
to the visualized mental picture.

Acquisition of forms that are more tangible occurs next. By adding
emotional feeling and etheric vitality, the influence of the visualized
mental picture extends and grows. However, the patient should maintain the proper emotional feeling during this process, namely, the
feeling of calm assurance that this effort of self-healing will be
successful.

Tenth Rule

As the waters bathe the form created, they are absorbed and used. The form increases in its strength; let the magician thus continue until the work suffices. Let the outer builders cease their labors then, and let the inner workers enter on their cycle.[12]

The "waters" refer to emotional feelings; "form," to the mental picture; "outer builders," to exercising conscious control; and "inner workers," to allowing the subconscious mind to control.

By maintaining both the proper emotional feeling and visualized mental picture, the feeling becomes associated with the picture and increases its influence. While the patient should consciously control these efforts on the mental and emotional levels, he should let his subconscious mind control the effort on the etheric level.

Eleventh Rule

Three things the worker with the law must now accomplish. First, ascertain the formula which will confine the lives within the ensphering wall; next, pronounce the words which will tell them what to do and where to carry that which has been made; and finally, to utter forth the mystic phrase which will save him from their work.[13]

The "formula" refers to a set of catch words. "Pronounce the words" refers to audibly speaking those catch words, and "utter forth the mystic phrase" refers to re-establishing the meditative state.

Three steps are needed to properly direct the subconscious mind: first, carefully choosing a set of catch words that embody (in the form of a rhythmic affirmation) the desired physical changes; second, directing the subconscious mind to heal the etheric body by audibly speaking those catch words, while maintaining the proper feeling and visualized mental picture; and third, relinquishing these etheric, emotional, and mental efforts by re-establishing the meditative state, in order to avoid becoming obsessed or driven by these efforts.

Twelfth Rule

The web pulsates. It contracts and expands. Let the magician seize the midway point and thus release those "prisoners of the planet" whose note is right and justly tuned to that which must be made.[14]

The "web" refers to the etheric body; "contracts," to inhalation; "expands," to exhalation; "midway point," to suspension of breath; and "prisoners of the planet," to etheric materials.

To be successful, it is important that this approach to self-healing be accompanied by organized rhythmic breathing. The fourth rule described three phases of the breathing cycle, and this twelfth rule describes the fourth phase—consequently, all four phases are utilized. During inhalation, the patient attains the meditative state, in which he becomes receptive to intuitive understanding from his causal body. During retention of breath, he receives an intuitive image of wholeness and then visualizes a corresponding mental picture. During exhalation, he establishes the proper emotional feeling and chooses a set of catch words that embody the desired physical changes. And during suspension of breath, he directs his subconscious mind to heal his physical body by audibly speaking those catch words, while maintaining the proper feeling and visualized mental picture. The technique is to repeat this four-phased cycle in a rhythmic way, over and over again. The patient may be intuitively guided to keep the same mental picture during each cycle, or to change that picture. When done properly, the subconscious mind will cause the appropriate etheric materials (such as prana) needed for the etheric healing to be drawn in and assimilated from the environment.

Thirteenth Rule

The magician must recognize the four; note in his work the shade of violet which they evidence, and thus construct the shadow. When this is so, the shadow clothes itself, and the four become the seven.[15]

The "four" refers to the four etheric subplanes of the physical plane; "shade of violet," to the quality of those etheric materials; "shadow," to the healed etheric body; "shadow clothes itself," to the process in which the healed etheric body automatically heals the dense physical body; and "four become the seven," to the extension of the physical healing from the four etheric subplanes to include all seven physical subplanes.

The patient must recognize the sources (such as his food, water, and air) of the etheric materials being assimilated, note the qualities (such as purity and vitality) of those materials, and ensure that those qualities are sufficiently healthful. Although the patient needs to direct his subconscious mind to heal his etheric body, he need not be concerned with his dense physical body, because the healed etheric body will automatically heal his dense physical body. In other words, a dense physical disorder is viewed as only a symptom of an etheric disorder—bringing wholeness to the latter will automatically bring wholeness to the former.

Fourteenth Rule

The sound swells out. The hour of danger to the soul courageous draweth near. The waters have not hurt the white creator and naught could drown nor drench him. Danger from fire and flame menaces now, and dimly yet the rising smoke is seen. Let him again, after the cycle of peace, call on the Solar Angel.[16]

The "sound swells out" refers to healing the etheric body according to the visualized mental picture; "hour of danger," to the appropriate moment for stopping the interference with the etheric body; "waters" refers to emotions; "drown or drench," to loss of emotional control; "danger from fire," to excessive interference with the etheric body; "rising smoke," to the beginning dense physical healing; "cycle of peace," to being in meditation; and "Solar Angel," to the causal body.

If the patient has successfully implemented the earlier rules, then he has begun the process of healing his etheric body according to the visualized mental picture, and maintained the proper emotional feeling by eliminating his undesirable personality reactions. Consequently, his dense physical body has also begun to heal. However, it is important for him to know when to stop this process, in order to avoid excessive interference with his etheric body. By re-establishing the meditative state during each inhalation of the breathing cycle, the patient can receive guidance from his causal body, which lets him know the appropriate moment of stopping.

Fifteenth Rule

The fires approach the shadow, yet burn it not. The fire sheath is completed. Let the magician chant the words that blend the fire and water.[17]

"The fires" refers to the etheric healing activity; "shadow," to the etheric body; "fire sheath is completed," to the etheric healing being completed; and "words that blend the fire and water," to the final directions given to the subconscious mind.

When the foregoing self-healing process no longer produces any changes in the etheric body, then the etheric body can be considered as being completely healed. The patient's final step is to direct his subconscious mind to maintain that etheric pattern, while having the feeling that this direction will be accomplished.

Stages of Chakra Evolution

Alice A. Bailey described a general process of evolution that she said was applicable to all types of form, including a solar system or planet on a macrocosmic level and a causal body, chakra, or single physical cell on a microcosmic level. She said that the process of evolution in all of these cases could be pictured with the same five symbols.[1] This appendix will illustrate her theory by showing how these specific symbols can represent the process of evolution for a major etheric chakra.

The five symbols, together with their interpretation as stages in the evolution for a given chakra, are as follows:

The circle: Corresponds to the stage in which the chakra is inactive. Table 7 on page 30 associates a specific quality of consciousness with each chakra. Thus, this symbol represents the stage in which the person does not express the quality associated with the given chakra.

The circle with the point in the center: Corresponds to the stage in which the chakra is active but undeveloped. The point of fire in the center signifies the beginning activity of the chakra. As discussed in Chapter 3, the purpose of meditation is to express deliberately a quality associated with a chakra that has not yet been developed, with the result of increasing the activity of that chakra. Thus, this symbol represents the stage of meditation.

The circle divided into two: Corresponds to the stage in which the chakra is both active and developed. The point of fire in the center has now become more intense and is able to radiate rays of fire to the periphery of the circle. As discussed in Chapters 4, 5, and 6, each of the major etheric chakras has at least one type of energy that can be radiated (perhaps via another chakra) after it has become developed. Thus, this symbol represents the stage of etheric radiation.

The circle divided into four: Corresponds to the stage in which the chakra is active, developed, and opened. Now the point of fire in the center radiates four rays of fire to the periphery, thus forming the equal-armed cross. These four rays signify that the chakra now has a fourth-dimensional quality. In the previous two stages, the chakra was actively functioning in the three dimensions of the physical plane. However, as discussed in Chapter 3, an opened etheric chakra is able to register sense impressions received by its emotional counterpart from the emotional plane, corresponding to a fourth dimension. Thus, this symbol represents the stage of psychic communication.

The swastika: Corresponds to the final stage in which the chakra is active, developed, opened, and energized by awakened kundalini energy. Now the equal-armed cross of the previous stage is rotating around the center point; the fire not only extends in four directions from the center to the periphery but circulates around the entire periphery. This symbol indicates that the chakra is fully energized, which is an effect of awakening the kundalini energy. Now all functions of the chakra can be performed in their most efficient and potent manner, implying that this symbol represents the completion of evolution for that chakra.

Experiences of Chakra Development

The last book of the Bible, called the Revelation of St. John the Divine, is written entirely in symbols and has two possible interpretations: *macrocosmic,* describing the process of evolution for humanity as a whole, and *microcosmic,* describing the process of evolution for an individual human being. The next two appendices will give a microcosmic interpretation that emphasizes the close relationship between the symbology of the Revelation and the information on chakra development presented in Chapter 3. Related versions of the microcosmic interpretation were given by Swami Yukteswar[1] and Cayce.[2]

One portion of the Revelation is concerned with a book having seven seals, in which a particular vision occurs as each seal is opened. This appendix will interpret the book as being the physical body, the seven seals as being the seven major etheric chakras, and each vision as being the experience that occurs when the associated chakra becomes developed.

First Experience

I saw when the Lamb opened one of the seals...a white horse: and he that sat on him had a bow; and a crown was given unto him: and he went forth conquering, and to conquer. (Rev. 6:1-2)

The sacral chakra ("first seal") becomes developed at birth, when the causal body (symbolized by the rider) acquires a new personality (symbolized by the horse) for functioning in the world. The color "white" symbolizes purity, indicating that the new personality has not yet been tarnished by worldly experiences. Two gifts are given at birth: a mind ("bow") having a penetrating intelligence; and a conscience, which is registered via the "crown" chakra. The purpose of being born is to "conquer" physical plane experience and thereby grow in wisdom.

Second Experience

When he had opened the second seal...there went out another horse that was red: and power was given to him that sat thereon to take peace from the earth, and that they should kill one another: and there was given unto him a great sword. (Rev. 6:3-4)

After the solar plexus chakra ("second seal") is developed, the person is able to experience intense emotions. The color of the horse is now red, which often represents the emotion of anger. The emotion of ambition is the "power" that enables a person to compete in the world and outdo other human beings ("kill one another"). Having intense emotions is like having "a great sword" that can be used to either dominate others or cause pain in oneself.

Third Experience

When he had opened the third seal...I beheld...a black horse; and he that sat on him had a pair of balances in his hand. And I heard a voice in the midst of the four beasts say, A measure of wheat for a penny, and three measures of barley for a penny; and see thou hurt not the oil and the wine. (Rev. 6:5-6)

After the heart chakra ("third seal") is developed, the person can be intuitively aware of the essential spiritual unity behind all physical forms. This intuition is conveyed by the inner "voice in the midst of the four beasts," the four beasts representing the fourfold personality (dense physical, etheric, emotional, and mental bodies). Consequently, the person can discern the relative value of the physical side of life (as symbolized by using a pair of balances to weigh wheat and barley) while not ignoring the spiritual side of life (as symbolized by not hurting the oil and wine). The color of the horse is now black, which is a color often worn in religious orders, indicating that the person does not overly value the superficial aspects of physical life.

Fourth Experience

> When he had opened the fourth seal, I...beheld a pale horse: and his name that sat on him was Death, and Hell followed with him. And power was given unto them over the fourth part of the earth, to kill with sword, and with hunger, and with death, and with the beasts of the earth. (Rev. 6:7-8)

After the throat chakra ("fourth seal") is developed, the person can more easily use his mental body to purify his emotional nature, the latter being a "fourth part" of his fourfold personality. This emotional purification can be achieved in several ways: by using the "sword" of understanding, by starving persistent undesirable habits, by refusing to express negative feelings, and by deliberately expressing other personality aspects ("beasts of the earth") through such means as physical exercises and intellectual pursuits. The color of the horse is now pale, which is the color of a sick or dying body.

Fifth Experience

> When he had opened the fifth seal, I saw under the altar the souls of them that were slain for the word of God, and for the testimony which they held: And they cried with a loud voice, saying, How long, O Lord, holy and true, dost thou

not judge and avenge our blood on them that dwell on the earth? And white robes were given unto every one of them; and it was said unto them, that they should rest yet for a little season, until their fellowservants also and their brethren, that should be killed as they were, should be fulfilled. (Rev. 6:9-11)

After the brow chakra ("fifth seal") is developed, the person is able to use his causal body to express intuitive wisdom easily. The causal body ("the altar") is the storehouse for the abstracted essence ("souls") that was gained by having purified ("slain for the word of God") many negative tendencies. Thus, each impurity, after being understood, becomes valued wisdom ("white robes were given unto every one of them"). Because the person still has some remaining self-centered goals, his mastery of the physical plane ("earth") will not be complete until his remaining selfishness is eliminated ("until their fellowservants also and their brethren, that should be killed as they were, should be fulfilled").

Sixth Experience

I beheld when he had opened the sixth seal, and, lo, there was a great earthquake; and the sun became black as sackcloth of hair, and the moon became as blood; And the stars of heaven fell unto the earth, even as a fig tree casteth her untimely figs, when she is shaken of a mighty wind. And the heaven departed as a scroll when it is rolled together; and every mountain and island were moved out of their places. And the kings of the earth, and the great men, and the rich men, and the chief captains, and the mighty men, and every bondman, and every free man, hid themselves in the dens and in the rocks of the mountains; And said to the mountains and rocks, Fall on us, and hide us from the face of him that sitteth on the throne, and from the wrath of the Lamb: For the great day of his wrath is come; and who shall be able to stand? (Rev. 6:12-17)

After the crown chakra ("sixth seal") is developed, the person can experience continuous self-awareness, meaning continuous detached awareness of his thoughts and feelings. Thus, he is able to reorient his life ("a great earthquake") by seeing the full truth about his remaining illusions, such as false ideals ("the sun became black," "moon became as blood," "stars of heaven fell," and "heaven departed"); material attainments and limited concepts ("every mountain and island were moved out of their place"); and various forms of pride and vanity ("the kings of the earth, and the great men, and the rich men, and the chief captains, and the mighty men, and every bondman, and every free man, hid themselves"). As a result of his continuous self-awareness, the person can proceed to eliminate all self-centeredness from his life ("for the great day of his wrath is come").

Seventh Experience

When he had opened the seventh seal, there was silence in heaven about the space of half an hour. And I saw the seven angels which stood before God; and to them were given seven trumpets. And another angel came and stood at the altar, having a golden censer; and there was given unto him much incense, that he should offer it with the prayers of all saints upon the golden altar which was before the throne. And the smoke of the incense, which came with the prayers of the saints, ascended up before God out of the angel's hand. And the angel took the censer, and filled it with fire of the altar, and cast it into the earth: and there were voices, and thunderings, and lightnings, and an earthquake. And the seven angels which had the seven trumpets prepared themselves to sound. (Rev. 8:1-6)

The basic chakra ("seventh seal") is said to be developed when the person has eliminated all self-centeredness, implying that he has found freedom from all inner conflict ("there was silence in heaven"). The person can now function as an integrated spiritual triad, causal body, and personality. Thus, his monadic will quality ("incense") can be transmitted through his spiritual triad ("another angel"), through his evolved causal body ("all saints upon the golden altar"), and through his crown chakra ("golden censer") to activate his basic chakra ("the earth"). Next his kundalini energy can awaken ("voices, and thunderings, and lightnings, and an earthquake") and rise to his crown chakra, thereby energizing each of his seven major etheric chakras ("the seven angels which had the seven trumpets prepared themselves to sound"). The person has completed his mastery over the physical plane.

Instructions for Attaining Higher Consciousness

Another portion of the last book of the Bible, the Revelation of St. John the Divine, includes seven symbolic instructions that are given by Jesus to the angels of seven churches. This appendix will interpret Jesus as being a person's monad, the seven churches as being the seven major etheric chakras, each angel as being the state of consciousness that results from developing the associated chakra, and the instruction given to each angel as being how a person can attain his next higher state of consciousness.

First Instruction

Unto the angel of the church of Ephesus write...I know thy works, and thy labour, and thy patience, and how thou canst not bear them which are evil: and thou hast tried them which say they are apostles, and are not, and hast found them liars: And hast borne, and hast patience, and for my name's sake hast laboured, and hast not fainted. Nevertheless I have somewhat against thee, because thou hast left thy first love. Remember therefore from whence thou art fallen, and repent, and do the first works; or else I will come unto thee quickly, and will remove thy candlestick out of his place, except thou repent. (Rev. 2:1-5)

This passage refers to the *sensual* state of consciousness—the first human state listed in Table 7, corresponding to a developed sacral chakra. In this state the person has a conscience, which means that he has glimpses of both self-awareness and spiritual will. As a result, he is able to examine himself and discern the presence of irresponsible activity ("canst not bear them which are evil") and self-deception ("hast tried them which say they are apostles, and are not, and hast found them liars").

Because the person in the sensual state is so identified with his physical body, he often forgets his conscience ("thou hast left thy first love"). But to achieve his next higher state of consciousness, he must remember to follow his conscience ("do the first works"). If he does not remember, then he can become so fixated with sensual gratification that his sacral chakra will cease to be active ("will remove thy candlestick out of his place"), which means that he will fall into a hypnotic trance.

Second Instruction

Unto the angel of the church in Smyrna write. . . I know thy works, and tribulation, and poverty, (but thou art rich) and I know the blasphemy of them which say they are Jews, and are not, but are the synagogue of Satan. Fear none of those things which thou shalt suffer: behold, the devil shall cast some of you into prison, that ye may be tried; and ye shall have tribulation ten days: be thou faithful unto death, and I will give thee a crown of life. (Rev. 2:8-10)

This second passage refers to the *aesthetic* state of consciousness, corresponding to a developed solar plexus chakra, which is the condition of an average or ordinary human being. In this state the person experiences much emotional "tribulation" and a sense of inner "poverty." He often attempts to maintain false illusions about himself ("the blasphemy of them which say they are Jews, and are not") by indulging in such emotions as pride and anger.

To attain his next higher state of consciousness, the person must learn to face those circumstances ("fear none of those things") that could tempt him to behave in an unethical or immoral way. After being tempted ("cast...into prison"), the person may feel "tried" and have "tribulation." But if he can remain "faithful" in the presence of those temptations as long as they last (or for "ten days," that term symbolizing completion), then he will gain a higher state ("crown of life").

Third Instruction

> To the angel of the church in Pergamos write...I know thy works, and where thou dwellest, even where Satan's seat is: and thou holdest fast my name, and hast not denied my faith, even in those days wherein Antipas was my faithful martyr, who was slain among you, where Satan dwelleth. But I have a few things against thee, because thou hast there them that hold the doctrine of Balaam, who taught Balac to cast a stumblingblock before the children of Israel, to eat things sacrificed unto idols, and to commit fornication. . . . Repent; or else I will come unto thee quickly, and will fight against them with the sword of my mouth. (Rev. 2:12-14, 16)

This passage refers to the *compassionate* state of consciousness, corresponding to a developed heart chakra. In this state the person experiences spiritual love ("holdeth fast my name"), which means that he perceives the spiritual nature of all beings, even when gross injustice is being committed by some of them ("even in those days wherein Antipas...was slain among you").

However, the person still has discordant thoughts and beliefs ("doctrine of Balaam"), which in turn cause his emotional body ("Balac") to be a "stumblingblock" by having such feelings as pride ("eat things sacrificed unto idols") and lust ("commit fornication"). To achieve his next higher state, the person must change those feelings ("repent") by using his discriminative intelligence ("sword of my mouth").

Fourth Instruction

Unto the angel of the church in Thyatira write...I know thy works, and charity, and service, and faith, and thy patience, and thy works; and the last to be more than the first. Notwithstanding I have a few things against thee, because thou sufferest that woman Jezebel, which calleth herself a prophetess, to teach and to seduce my servants to commit fornication, and to eat things sacrificed unto idols. And I gave her space to repent of her fornication; and she repented not. Behold, I will cast her into a bed, and them that commit adultery with her into great tribulation, except they repent of their deeds. And I will kill her children with death; and all the churches shall know that I am he which searcheth the reins and hearts: and I will give unto every one of you according to your works. (Rev. 2:18-23)

This fourth passage refers to the *creative* state of consciousness, corresponding to a developed throat chakra. In this state the person's mental body is able to express concrete thinking in a creative way, thereby enabling him to perform "works, and charity, and service."

However, the person still allows discord in his concrete thinking ("Jezebel") to cause ("to teach and to seduce") his feelings ("servants") to express lust ("commit fornication") and pride ("eat things sacrificed unto idols"). To achieve his next higher state, his thoughts must change ("repent of their deeds"), which in turn will change his feelings ("kill her children with death"). The person can make this change by first observing his concrete thoughts and feelings in a detached and objective way ("searcheth the reins and hearts") and then allowing his wisdom to appraise and guide his concrete thinking ("I will give unto every one of you according to your works").

Fifth Instruction

Unto the angel of the church in Sardis write...I know thy works, that thou hast a name that thou livest, and art dead. Be watchful, and strengthen the things which remain, that are ready to die: for I have not found thy works perfect before God. Remember therefore how thou hast received and heard, and hold fast, and repent. If therefore thou shalt not watch, I will come on thee as a thief, and thou shalt not know what hour I will come upon thee. (Rev. 3:1-3)

This passage refers to the *intuitive* state of consciousness, corresponding to a developed brow chakra. In this state the person's causal body is able to express wisdom in a strong and clear way, which in turn can control his personality. Thus, he "livest" as a causal body, but is "dead" as a personality.

Because wisdom is based upon past experience, it is limited ("I have not found thy works perfect before God"). To achieve his next higher state, the person should become detached and objective ("watchful") towards his wisdom, and then allow the insights of his spiritual mind to eliminate those "things...that are ready to die." But if his self-awareness is allowed to lapse ("if therefore thou shalt not watch"), then he may miss the opportunity of receiving an insight ("thou shalt not know what hour I will come upon thee").

Sixth Instruction

To the angel of the church in Philadelphia write...I know thy works: behold, I have set before thee an open door, and no man can shut it; for thou hast a little strength, and hast kept my word, and hast not denied my name. Behold, I will make them of the synagogue of Satan, which say they are Jews, and are not, but do lie; behold, I will make them to come and worship before thy feet, and to know that I have loved thee. Because thou hast kept the word of my patience, I also will keep thee from the hour of temptation, which shall come upon all the world, to try them that dwell upon the earth. Behold, I come quickly: hold that fast which thou hast, that no man take thy crown. (Rev. 3:7-11)

This passage refers to the *self-consciousness* state, corresponding to a developed crown chakra. Because of the person's persistence ("strength"), purification ("hast kept my word"), and compassion ("hast not denied my name"), his etheric spine has become an "open door," meaning that all etheric webs separating his etheric chakras have been dissipated. Consequently, he can experience continuous self-awareness, which means continuous detached awareness of his abstract thoughts, concrete thoughts, emotional feelings, and physical behavior. Thus, he can be aware of his remaining illusions (those aspects "which say they are Jews, and are not, but do lie") and then gain additional wisdom ("worship") by understanding them. He also can be detached with respect to all forms of "temptation" existing in the world.

To achieve his next higher state, the person must maintain his self-awareness ("hold that fast which thou hast"), so that no remaining illusion can cause him to regress back into a lower state of consciousness ("that no man take thy crown").

Seventh Instruction

Unto the angel of the church of the Laodiceans write...I know thy works, that thou art neither cold nor hot: I would thou wert cold or hot. So then because thou are lukewarm, and neither cold nor hot, I will spue thee out of my mouth. Because thou sayest, I am rich, and increased with goods, and have need of nothing; and knowest not that thou are wretched, and miserable, and poor, and blind, and naked: I counsel thee to buy of me gold tried in the fire, that thou mayest be rich; and white raiment, that thou mayest be clothed, and that the shame of thy nakedness do not appear; and anoint thine eyes with eyesalve, that thou mayest see. As many as I love, I rebuke and chasten: be zealous therefore, and repent. Behold, I stand at the door, and knock: if any man hear my voice, and open the door, I will come in to him, and will sup with him, and he with me. (Rev. 3:14-20)

This final passage refers to the *objective consciousness* state, corresponding to a developed basic chakra. In this state the person has eliminated all self-centered activity and instead expresses the spiritual will. Consequently, he is "rich," is "increased with goods," and has "need of nothing." By having completed his evolution in the human kingdom of nature, the person is ready to begin a new cycle of evolution in the kingdom of souls. His next task is to achieve a still higher state of consciousness, sometimes called "monadic consciousness," which is experienced as conscious union with the monad.

The person is not yet ready to experience conscious union with the monad ("I will spue thee out of my mouth"), because of the lack of intensity in his "works": he now expresses the spiritual will ("thou are lukewarm"), but does not directly express the more intense monadic will quality ("I would thou wert cold or hot"). In comparison with his potential, he presently is "wretched, and miserable, and poor, and blind, and naked." To achieve his next higher state, he must gain new wisdom ("buy...gold tried in the fire"), further spiritualize his consciousness ("buy...white raiment"), and become sensitive to still higher impressions ("anoint thine eyes with eyesalve, that thou mayest see"). Although glimpses of the monadic will quality can be sensed ("I stand at the door, and knock"), the person must make an effort ("open the door") in order to fully register and express this higher impulse. If he does so, then he will experience conscious union with the monad ("I will come in to him, and will sup with him, and he with me").

Notes

Chapter 1: Inner Constitution

1. For more comprehensive treatments of the inner constitution, the reader is referred to A. E. Powell, *The Etheric Double; The Astral Body; The Mental Body; The Causal Body and the Ego;* and A. Jurriaanse, *Bridges.* For full publication data, see title listing in the Bibliography.
2. A. Jurriaanse, *Bridges* (Cape, South Africa: Sun Centre, 1978), 77-79.
3. A. E. Powell, *The Astral Body* (1927; reprint; Wheaton, IL: Theosophical Publishing House, 1978), 23-30.
4. A. E. Powell, *The Mental Body* (1927; reprint; Wheaton, IL: Theosophical Publishing House, 1975), 1-22.
5. A. A. Bailey, *A Treatise on Cosmic Fire* (1925; reprint; New York: Lucis Publishing Company, 1977), 707-714.
6. A. A. Bailey, *The Rays and the Initiations* (1960; reprint; New York: Lucis Publishing Company, 1976), 460-461.
7. A. Besant, *A Study in Consciousness* (1904; reprint; Adyar, India: Theosophical Publishing House, 1975), 10-12.
8. Besant, *A Study in Consciousness*, 41.
9. Besant, *A Study in Consciousness*, 39-40.
10. Besant, *A Study in Consciousness*, 45-49.
11. A. A. Bailey, *Esoteric Astrology* (1951; reprint; New York: Lucis Publishing Company, 1979), 580-587.
12. A. A. Bailey, *Glamour: A World Problem*, (1950; reprint; New York: Lucis Publishing Company, 1971), 2-5.

13. Besant, *A Study in Consciousness*, 46-53.
14. Jurriaanse, *Bridges*, 145-146.
15. A. A. Bailey, *Esoteric Psychology*, vol. 2 (1942; reprint; New York: Lucis Publishing Company, 1975), 71-72.
16. C. W. Leadbeater, *A Textbook of Theosophy* (1912; reprint; Adyar, India: Theosophical Publishing House, 1962), 112-113.

Chapter 2: Etheric Chakras

1. A. A. Bailey, *Esoteric Healing* (1953; reprint; New York: Lucis Publishing Company, 1977), 72.
2. Bailey, *Esoteric Healing*, 144-189; A. A. Bailey, *A Treatise on White Magic* (1934; reprint; New York: Lucis Publishing Company, 1974), 283-288.
3. A. A. Bailey, *The Rays and the Initiations* (1960; reprint; New York: Lucis Publishing Company, 1976), 450.
4. H. Motoyama, *Science and the Evolution of Consciousness* (Brookline, MA: Autumn Press, 1978), 90-93, 143-144.
5. C. W. Leadbeater, *The Chakras* (1927; reprint; Wheaton, IL: Theosophical Publishing House, 1977), 4-5.
6. A. A. Bailey, *Telepathy and the Etheric Vehicle* (1950; reprint; New York: Lucis Publishing Company, 1975), 146.
7. Bailey, *Esoteric Healing*, 461.
8. D. V. Tansley, *Radionics and the Subtle Anatomy of Man* (1972; reprint; Essex, England: Health Science Press, 1980), 29.
9. A. A. Bailey, *Esoteric Psychology*, vol. 2 (1942; reprint; New York: Lucis Publishing Company, 1975), 589.
10. Bailey, *Esoteric Healing*, 140-143.
11. E. C. Chaney, "Man—Master of Destiny or Victim of Fate," *Astara's Book of Life* 2, no. 6 (1966), 11.
12. A. Gardner, *Vital Magnetic Healing* (3rd ed.; London: Theosophical Publishing House, 1948), 19.
13. Bailey, *Esoteric Healing*, 618.
14. Bailey, *Esoteric Healing*, 159-160, 213-214.

Chapter 3: States of Consciousness

1. J. Roberts, *The Nature of Personal Reality: A Seth Book* (Englewood Cliffs, NJ: Prentice-Hall, 1974), 170-178.
2. Roberts, *The Nature of Personal Reality*, 162-164.
3. P. D. Ouspensky, *The Psychology of Man's Possible Evolution* (1954; reprint; New York: Alfred A. Knopf, 1972), 34.
4. Ouspensky, *The Psychology of Man's Possible Evolution*, 35.
5. Ouspensky, *The Psychology of Man's Possible Evolution*, 36-37.
6. Ouspensky, *The Psychology of Man's Possible Evolution*, 19-20.
7. A. A. Bailey, *Esoteric Psychology*, vol. 1 (1936; reprint; New York: Lucis Publishing Company, 1975), 422-428.
8. A. E. Powell, *The Causal Body and the Ego* (1928; reprint; Wheaton, IL: Theosophical Publishing House, 1978), 267-277, 309-321.
9. A. A. Bailey, *Esoteric Healing* (1953; reprint; New York: Lucis Publishing Company, 1977), 469-470, 500-501, 506.
10. A. A. Bailey, *Esoteric Psychology*, vol. 2 (1942; reprint; New York: Lucis Publishing Company, 1975), 25-26.
11. A. A. Bailey, *Initiation, Human and Solar* (1922; reprint; New York: Lucis Publishing Company, 1974), 82-84.
12. A. A. Bailey, *Letters on Occult Meditation* (1922; reprint; New York: Lucis Publishing Company, 1974), 27-28, 75.
13. A. A. Bailey, *The Rays and the Initiations* (1960; reprint; New York: Lucis Publishing Company, 1976), 687-692.
14. Bailey, *The Rays and the Initiations*, 692-703.
15. Bailey, *The Rays and the Initiations*, 703-718.
16. Bailey, *Esoteric Healing*, 186-187, 202; A. A. Bailey, *A Treatise on White Magic* (1934; reprint; New York: Lucis Publishing Company, 1974), 591-592. These references describe seven etheric webs. In addition to the six webs mentioned in the text, there is a web on top of the head which separates the etheric crown chakra from its counterpart on the emotional plane. This latter web will be considered in the section on chakra opening.
17. Bailey, *Esoteric Healing*, 181-182.
18. Bailey, *Esoteric Healing*, 186.
19. Bailey, *Esoteric Healing*, 194-195.

20. E. C. Chaney, "The Upraised Serpent: Guardian of the Golden Fleece," *Astara's Book of Life* 1, no. 13 (1966), 1-4.
21. Bailey, *Letters on Occult Meditation*, 74-75; Bailey, *Esoteric Psychology*, vol. 2, 530, 594-595.
22. Bailey, *Esoteric Healing*, 183-184.
23. A. A. Bailey, *A Treatise on Cosmic Fire* (1925; reprint; New York: Lucis Publishing Company, 1977), 124-125, 134-140, 183-185, 1159.
24. Bailey, *Esoteric Healing*, 200, 581.
25. Bailey, *A Treatise on Cosmic Fire*, 126, 1160; Bailey, *The Rays and the Initiations*, 356.
26. Bailey, *Esoteric Psychology*, vol. 2, 527-530.
27. Bailey, *A Treatise on White Magic*, 590.
28. Bailey, *Esoteric Healing*, 212-213.
29. Foundation for Inner Peace, *A Course in Miracles*, vol. 1 (Huntington Station, NY: Coleman Graphics, 1975), 570.
30. H. Chaudhuri, *Integral Yoga* (1965; reprint; San Francisco: California Institute of Asian Studies, 1970), 67-73.
31. A. A. Bailey, *From Intellect to Intuition* (1932; reprint; New York: Lucis Publishing Company, 1974), 199-234.
32. J. S. Goldsmith, *The Art of Meditation* (New York: Harper and Row, 1956), 26.
33. P. D. Ouspensky, *The Fourth Way* (1957; reprint; New York: Random House, 1971), 105-133.
34. J. Krishnamurti, *Freedom from the Known* (New York: Harper and Row, 1969), 115-116.
35. N. Thera, *The Heart of Buddhist Meditation* (1962; reprint; York Beach, ME: Samuel Weiser, 1973), 92-99.
36. Chaudhuri, *Integral Yoga*, 93-99, 130-132.
37. Bailey, *Esoteric Healing*, 185.
38. Bailey, *A Treatise on White Magic*, 590-591.
39. Bailey, *The Rays and the Initiations*, 643-653.
40. Bailey, *A Treatise on White Magic*, 501.
41. M. P. Hall, *Man, Grand Symbol of the Mysteries* (6th ed.; Los Angeles: Philosophical Research Society, 1972), 107-119.
42. A. Besant, *A Study in Consciousness* (1904; reprint; Adyar, India: Theosophical Publishing House, 1975), 53.
43. Bailey, *Esoteric Psychology*, vol. 2, 220-221, 231-237.

44. Bailey, *Esoteric Psychology*, vol. 2, 417-421.
45. Bailey, *From Intellect to Intuition*, 104, 229, 232.
46. E. Green and A. Green, *Beyond Biofeedback* (New York: Dell, 1977), 21-41.
47. Bailey, *Esoteric Psychology*, vol. 2, 483-484.
48. J. Krishnamurti, *Commentaries on Living, Third Series* (1960; reprint; Wheaton, IL: Theosophical Publishing House, 1970), 6-9.
49. A. A. Bailey, *The Light of the Soul* (1927; reprint; New York: Lucis Publishing Company, 1978), 21-22.
50. Bailey, *From Intellect to Intuition*, 229.
51. A. Jurriaanse, *Bridges* (Cape, South Africa: Sun Centre, 1978), 87-88.
52. C. W. Leadbeater, *The Chakras* (1927; reprint; Wheaton, IL: Theosophical Publishing House, 1977), 89.
53. A. A. Bailey, *The Externalisation of the Hierarchy* (1957; reprint; New York: Lucis Publishing Company, 1976), 8-9.
54. Leadbeater, *The Chakras*, 49-50.
55. Bailey, *A Treatise on White Magic*, 500-501.
56. Bailey, *A Treatise on White Magic*, 501.
57. Bailey, *The Light of the Soul*, 38-42, 211-213.
58. Bailey, *Esoteric Psychology*, vol. 2, 66.
59. Bailey, *Initiation, Human and Solar*, 86-87.
60. Green and Green, *Beyond Biofeedback*, 316-325.
61. Bailey, *A Treatise on White Magic*, 175, 181, 304.
62. Bailey, *The Externalisation of the Hierarchy*, 11-12.
63. Bailey, *Esoteric Psychology*, vol. 2, 475-478, 583, 590.
64. Bailey, *Esoteric Psychology*, vol. 2, 579-591.

Chapter 4: Pranic Healing

1. Yogi Ramacharaka, *The Science of Psychic Healing* (1909; reprint; Chicago: Yogi Publication Society, 1937), 37.
2. H. P. Blavatsky, *The Secret Doctrine*, 1905; quoted by A. E. Powell, *The Etheric Double* (1925; reprint; Wheaton, IL: Theosophical Publishing House, 1979), 10-11.
3. A. A. Bailey, *Esoteric Healing* (1953; reprint; New York: Lucis Publishing Company, 1977), 428-429.

4. C. W. Leadbeater, *The Chakras* (1927; reprint; Wheaton, IL: Theosophical Publishing House, 1977), 42-54.

5. J. M. Tyberg, *The Language of the Gods* (Los Angeles: East-West Cultural Centre, 1970), 102-103.

6. A. A. Bailey, *The Light of the Soul* (1927; reprint; New York: Lucis Publishing Company, 1978), 329-330.

7. C. W. Leadbeater, *The Chakras*, 55-61.

8. A. A. Bailey, *Discipleship in the New Age*, vol. 1 (1944; reprint; New York: Lucis Publishing Company, 1976), 752.

9. Bailey, *Esoteric Healing*, 194-199.

10. Bailey, *Esoteric Healing*, 283-284.

11. Bailey, *Esoteric Healing*, 206, 645.

12. Bailey, *Esoteric Healing*, 207, 526, 555, 626-627.

13. Bailey, *Esoteric Healing*, 575.

14. A. Gardner, *Vital Magnetic Healing* (3rd ed.; London: Theosophical Publishing House, 1948), 13.

15. Bailey, *Esoteric Healing*, 275.

16. Bailey, *Esoteric Healing*, 287.

17. Leadbeater, *The Chakras*, 67-68.

18. Bailey, *Esoteric Healing*, 578-579.

19. H. Naylor, unpublished lecture recorded on tape, San Jose, California, December 1980. Used by permission.

20. E. C. Chaney, "The Birth of the Third Eye," *Astara's Book of Life* 2, no. 8 (1966), 18.

21. Bailey, *Esoteric Healing*, 580.

22. Leadbeater, *The Chakras*, 56-58, 66-67.

23. Bailey, *Esoteric Healing*, 553.

24. Bailey, *Esoteric Healing*, 606.

25. Bailey, *Esoteric Healing*, 27.

26. H. Edwards, *The Healing Intelligence* (1965; reprint; London: The Healer Publishing Co. Ltd., 1974), 137.

27. G. W. Meek, "The Role of 'Discarnate Entities' In Healing" in *Healers and the Healing Process*, ed., G. W. Meek (Wheaton, IL: Theosophical Publishing House, 1977), 270-284.

28. A. A. Bailey, *A Treatise on White Magic* (1934; reprint; New York: Lucis Publishing Company, 1974), 578.

29. H. Naylor, unpublished lecture recorded on tape, San Jose, California, December 1980.
30. Bailey, *Esoteric Healing*, 329.

Chapter 5: Telepathic Healing

1. A. Jurriaanse, *Bridges* (Cape, South Africa: Sun Centre, 1978), 343.
2. A. A. Bailey, *Telepathy and the Etheric Vehicle* (1950; reprint; New York: Lucis Publishing Company, 1975), 12, 19, 21, 117-118.
3. A. A. Bailey, *Discipleship in the New Age*, vol. 2 (1955; reprint; New York: Lucis Publishing Company, 1972), 622-626, 753.
4. Bailey, *Telepathy and the Etheric Vehicle*, 9, 18, 20, 67-68, 117.
5. Bailey, *Telepathy and the Etheric Vehicle*, 9, 18, 20.
6. Bailey, *Telepathy and the Etheric Vehicle*, 9, 17, 20, 116.
7. Bailey, *Telepathy and the Etheric Vehicle*, 16, 116.
8. Bailey, *Discipleship in the New Age*, vol. 2, 535-536.
9. Bailey, *Discipleship in the New Age*, vol. 2, 113-114.
10. A. Besant, *Thought Power* (1903; reprint; Adyar, India: Theosophical Publishing House, 1969), 31-37.
11. R. B. Ball, *The Pathways of Healing* (Stanford, CA: R. B. Ball, 1978), 17, 26.
12. E. C. Chaney, "Techniques for the Initiate," *Astara's Book of Life* 6, no. 21 (1982), 17.
13. A. A. Bailey, *A Treatise on White Magic* (1934; reprint; New York: Lucis Publishing Company, 1974), 205-206.
14. Bailey, *Telepathy and the Etheric Vehicle*, 29.
15. C. W. Leadbeater, *The Hidden Side of Things* (1913; reprint; Adyar, India: Theosophical Publishing House, 1977), 477-479.
16. Besant, *Thought Power*, 113.
17. G. Hodson, *The Kingdom of the Gods* (1952; reprint; Adyar, India: Theosophical Publishing House, 1970), 197.
18. A. A. Bailey, *Discipleship in the New Age*, vol. 1 (1944; reprint; New York: Lucis Publishing Company, 1976), 65.
19. Bailey, *Discipleship in the New Age*, vol. 1, 67.
20. Bailey, *Telepathy and the Etheric Vehicle*, 12, 87.

21. Bailey, *Telepathy and the Etheric Vehicle*, 9.
22. Yogi Ramacharaka, *The Science of Psychic Healing* (1909; reprint; Chicago: Yogi Publication Society, 1937), 26-32.
23. Neville, *Resurrection* (1966; reprint; Santa Monica, CA: De Vorss, 1971), 26-30.
24. Yogi Ramacharaka, *The Science of Psychic Healing*, 160-161.
25. From the book *Amazing Secrets of Psychic Healing* by Benjamin O. Bibb and Joseph J. Weed, © 1976 by Parker Publishing Co. Published by Parker Publishing Co., Inc., West Nyack, NY.
26. Bailey, *Telepathy and the Etheric Vehicle*, 88.

Chapter 6: Radiatory Healing

1. A. A. Bailey, *A Treatise on Cosmic Fire* (1925; reprint; New York: Lucis Publishing Company, 1977), 823.
2. C. W. Leadbeater, *Man Visible and Invisible* (1902; reprint; Wheaton, IL: Theosophical Publishing House, 1969), 54, 119-120. According to Table 7, the arhat has a developed crown chakra.
3. A. A. Bailey, *A Treatise on Cosmic Fire*, 816.
4. A. A. Bailey, *A Treatise on Cosmic Fire*, 538-544, 1110-1116.
5. A. A. Bailey, *Esoteric Healing* (1953; reprint; New York: Lucis Publishing Company, 1977), 653-658.
6. A. A. Bailey, *Telepathy and the Etheric Vehicle* (1950; reprint; New York: Lucis Publishing Company, 1975), 97, 173.
7. A. E. Powell, *The Causal Body and the Ego* (1928; reprint; Wheaton, IL: Theosophical Publishing House, 1978), 189.
8. Bailey, *Esoteric Healing*, 547.
9. Bailey, *A Treatise on Cosmic Fire*, 863.
10. Bailey, *Esoteric Healing*, 554.
11. Bailey, *Esoteric Healing*, 656.
12. A. A. Bailey, *The Rays and the Initiations* (1960; reprint; New York: Lucis Publishing Company, 1976), 689-690; Bailey, *Esoteric Healing*, 547, 577, 581.
13. Powell, *The Causal Body and the Ego*, 270; A. A. Bailey, *Discipleship in the New Age*, vol. 2 (1955; reprint; New York: Lucis Publishing Company, 1972), 244.

14. Bailey, *Esoteric Healing*, 551.
15. I. B. Bentov, *Stalking the Wild Pendulum* (New York: E. P. Dutton, 1977), 18-19.
16. Bailey, *Esoteric Healing*, 604-605.
17. C. W. Leadbeater, *Telepathy and Mind-Cure* (London: Theosophical Publishing House, 1926), 19.
18. J. S. Goldsmith, *The Art of Spiritual Healing* (New York: Harper and Row, 1959), 188-189.
19. Foundation for Inner Peace, *A Course in Miracles*, vol. 2 (Huntington Station, NY: Coleman Graphics, 1975), 347.
20. Bailey, *Telepathy and the Etheric Vehicle*, 175.
21. E. Green and A. Green, *Beyond Biofeedback* (New York: Dell, 1977), 72-117.
22. Bailey, *Esoteric Healing*, 603-604.
23. Bailey, *Esoteric Healing*, 655-656.
24. A. A. Bailey, *A Treatise on White Magic* (1934; reprint; New York: Lucis Publishing Company, 1974), 576.
25. Bailey, *Esoteric Healing*, 656.
26. Bailey, *A Treatise on White Magic*, 576.
27. A. A. Bailey, *Discipleship in the New Age*, vol. 1 (1944; reprint; New York: Lucis Publishing Company, 1976), 753-756.

Chapter 7: Conclusions

1. H. Motoyama, "Physiological Measurements and New Instrumentation" in *Healers and the Healing Process*, ed., G. W. Meek (Wheaton, IL: Theosophical Publishing House, 1977), 147-155.
2. B. Grad, "Laboratory Evidence of the 'Laying-on-of-Hands'" in *The Dimensions of Healing* (Los Altos, CA: Academy of Parapsychology and Medicine, 1972), 29-34.
3. Sister M. J. Smith, "The Influence of Enzyme Growth by the 'Laying-on-of-Hands'" in *The Dimensions of Healing* (Los Altos, CA: Academy of Parapsychology and Medicine, 1972), 110-120.
4. R. N. Miller, "Methods of Detecting and Measuring Healing Energies" in *Future Science*, eds., J. White and S. Krippner (Garden City, NY: Anchor-Doubleday, 1977), 431-444.

Appendix I

1. A. A. Bailey, *Esoteric Healing* (1953; reprint; New York: Lucis Publishing Company, 1977), 706.
2. Bailey, *Esoteric Healing*, 706.
3. Bailey, *Esoteric Healing*, 706-707.
4. Bailey, *Esoteric Healing*, 707-708.
5. Bailey, *Esoteric Healing*, 708.
6. Bailey, *Esoteric Healing*, 709.
7. Bailey, *Esoteric Healing*, 710.
8. Bailey, *Esoteric Healing*, 711.
9. Bailey, *Esoteric Healing*, 712.
10. A. A. Bailey, *Esoteric Psychology*, vol. 1 (1936; reprint; New York: Lucis Publishing Company, 1975), 316, 411-430.

Appendix II

1. A. A. Bailey, *A Treatise on Cosmic Fire* (1925; reprint; New York: Lucis Publishing Company, 1977), 996-997.
2. A. A. Bailey, *A Treatise on White Magic* (1934; reprint; New York: Lucis Publishing Company, 1974), 453.
3. Bailey, *A Treatise on Cosmic Fire*, 997.
4. Bailey, *A Treatise on Cosmic Fire*, 998.
5. Bailey, *A Treatise on Comsic Fire*, 1000.
6. Bailey, *A Treatise on Cosmic Fire*, 1002.
7. Bailey, *A Treatise on Cosmic Fire*, 1004.
8. Bailey, *A Treatise on Cosmic Fire*, 1008.
9. Bailey, *A Treatise on Cosmic Fire*, 1013.
10. Bailey, *A Treatise on Cosmic Fire*, 1014.
11. Bailey, *A Treatise on Cosmic Fire*, 1017.
12. Bailey, *A Treatise on Cosmic Fire*, 1017.
13. Bailey, *A Treatise on Cosmic Fire*, 1020.
14. Bailey, *A Treatise on Cosmic Fire*, 1023.
15. Bailey, *A Treatise on Cosmic Fire*, 1024.
16. Bailey, *A Treatise on Cosmic Fire*, 1024-1025.
17. Bailey, *A Treatise on Cosmic Fire*, 1026.

Appendix III

1. A. A. Bailey, *A Treatise on Cosmic Fire* (1925; reprint; New York: Lucis Publishing Company, 1977), 159-161, 171-172.

Appendix IV

1. Swami Yukteswar, *The Holy Science* (1949; reprint; Los Angeles: Self-Realization Fellowship, 1977).
2. *A Commentary on the Book of the Revelation Based on a Study of Twenty-four Psychic Discourses by Edgar Cayce* (1945; rev. ed; Virginia Beach, VA: A.R.E. Press, 1968).

Bibliography

Bailey, A. A. *Discipleship in the New Age*, vol. 1. 1944. Reprint. New York: Lucis Publishing Company, 1976.

_____.*Discipleship in the New Age*, vol. 2. 1955. Reprint. New York: Lucis Publishing Company, 1972.

_____.*Esoteric Astrology*. 1951. Reprint. New York: Lucis Publishing Company, 1979.

_____.*Esoteric Healing*. 1953. Reprint. New York: Lucis Publishing Company, 1977.

_____.*Esoteric Psychology*, vol. 1. 1936. Reprint. New York: Lucis Publishing Company, 1975.

_____.*Esoteric Psychology*, vol. 2. 1942. Reprint. New York: Lucis Publishing Company, 1975.

_____.*The Externalisation of the Hierarchy*. 1957. Reprint. New York: Lucis Publishing Company, 1976.

_____.*From Intellect to Intuition*. 1932. Reprint. New York: Lucis Publishing Company, 1974.

_____.*Glamour: A World Problem*. 1950. Reprint. New York: Lucis Publishing Company, 1971.

_____.*Initiation, Human and Solar*. 1922. Reprint. New York: Lucis Publishing Company, 1974.

_____.*Letters on Occult Meditation*. 1922. Reprint. New York: Lucis Publishing Company, 1974.

_____.*The Light of the Soul*. 1927. Reprint. New York: Lucis Publishing Company, 1978.

_____.*The Rays and the Initiations.* 1960. Reprint. New York: Lucis Publishing Company, 1976.

_____.*Telepathy and the Etheric Vehicle.* 1950. Reprint. New York: Lucis Publishing Company, 1975.

_____.*A Treatise on Cosmic Fire.* 1925. Reprint. New York: Lucis Publishing Company, 1977.

_____.*A Treatise on White Magic.* 1934. Reprint. New York: Lucis Publishing Company, 1974.

Ball, R. B. *The Pathways of Healing.* Stanford, CA: R. B. Ball, 1978.

Beasley, V. *Subtle-Body Healing.* Boulder Creek, CA: University of the Trees Press, 1979.

Bentov, I. *Stalking the Wild Pendulum.* New York: E. P. Dutton, 1977.

Besant, A. *A Study in Consciousness.* 1904. Reprint. Adyar, India: Theosophical Publishing House, 1975.

_____.*Thought Power.* 1903. Reprint. Adyar, India: Theosophical Publishing House, 1969.

Bibb, B. O., and J. J. Weed. *Amazing Secrets of Psychic Healing.* West Nyack, NY: Parker Publishing Company, 1976.

Chaney, E. C. "The Birth of the Third Eye," *Astara's Book of Life* 2, no. 8 (1966).

_____."Man—Master of Destiny or Victim of Fate," *Astara's Book of Life* 2, no. 6 (1966).

_____."Man—The Measure of All Things," *Astara's Book of Life* 1, no. 10 (1965).

_____."Techniques for the Initiate," *Astara's Book of Life* 6, no. 21 (1982).

_____."Treasures on the Tree of Life," *Astara's Book of Life* 2, no. 9 (1966).

_____."The Upraised Serpent: Guardian of the Golden Fleece," *Astara's Book of Life* 1, no. 13 (1966).

Chaudhuri, H. *Integral Yoga.* 1965. Reprint. San Francisco: California Institute of Asian Studies, 1970.

A Commentary on the Book of the Revelation Based on a Study of Twenty-Four Psychic Discourses by Edgar Cayce. 1945. Rev. ed. Virginia Beach, VA: A.R.E. Press, 1968.

The Dimensions of Healing. Los Altos, CA: Academy of Parapsychology and Medicine, 1972.

Edwards, H. *The Healing Intelligence*. 1965. Reprint. London: The Healer Publishing Co. Ltd., 1974.

Foundation for Inner Peace. *A Course in Miracles*, vol. 1, 2, and 3. Huntington Station, NY: Coleman Graphics, 1975.

Gardner, A. *Vital Magnetic Healing*. 3rd ed. London: Theosophical Publishing House, 1948.

Goldsmith, J. S. *The Art of Meditation*. New York: Harper and Row, 1956.

————.*The Art of Spiritual Healing*. New York: Harper and Row, 1959.

Green, E., and A. Green. *Beyond Biofeedback*. New York: Dell, 1977.

Hall, M. P. *Man, Grand Symbol of the Mysteries*. 6th ed. Los Angeles: Philosophical Research Society, 1972.

Hodson, G. *The Kingdom of the Gods*. 1952. Reprint. Adyar, India: Theosophical Publishing House, 1970.

Jurriaanse, A. *Bridges*. Cape, South Africa: Sun Centre, 1978.

Krishnamurti, J. *Commentaries on Living, Third Series*. 1960. Reprint. Wheaton, IL: Theosophical Publishing House, 1970.

————.*Freedom from the Known*. New York: Harper and Row, 1969.

Leadbeater, C. W. *The Chakras*. 1927. Reprint. Wheaton, IL: Theosophical Publishing House, 1977.

————.*The Hidden Side of Things*. 1913. Reprint. Adyar, India: Theosophical Publishing House, 1977.

————.*Man Visible and Invisible*. 1902. Reprint. Wheaton, IL: Theosophical Publishing House, 1969.

————.*Telepathy and Mind-Cure*. London: Theosophical Publishing House, 1926.

————.*A Textbook of Theosophy*. 1912. Reprint. Adyar, India: Theosophical Publishing House, 1962.

LeBaron, R. *Hormones*. New York: Bobbs-Merill, 1972.

Meek, G. W., ed. *Healers and the Healing Process*. Wheaton, IL: Theosophical Publishing House, 1977.

Motoyama, H. *Science and the Evolution of Consciousness*. Brookline, MA: Autumn Press, 1978.

Neville. *Resurrection*. 1966. Reprint. Santa Monica, CA: De Vorss, 1971.

Ouspensky, P. D. *The Fourth Way*. 1957. Reprint. New York: Random House, 1971.

————.*The Psychology of Man's Possible Evolution*. 1954. Reprint. New York: Alfred A. Knopf, 1972.

Powell, A. E. *The Astral Body.* 1927. Reprint. Wheaton, IL: Theosophical Publishing House, 1978.

―――.*The Causal Body and the Ego.* 1928. Reprint. Wheaton, IL: Theosophical Publishing House, 1978.

―――.*The Etheric Double.* 1925. Reprint. Wheaton, IL: Theosophical Publishing House, 1979.

―――.*The Mental Body.* 1927. Reprint. Wheaton, IL: Theosophical Publishing House, 1975.

Ramacharaka, Yogi. *The Science of Psychic Healing.* 1909. Reprint. Chicago: Yogi Publication Society, 1937.

Roberts, J. *The Nature of Personal Reality: A Seth Book.* Englewood Cliffs, NJ: Prentice-Hall, 1974.

Saraydarian, H. *Cosmos in Man.* Agoura, CA: The Aquarian Educational Group, 1973.

Schwarz, J. *Human Energy Systems.* New York: E. P. Dutton, 1980.

Tansley, D. V. *Radionics and the Subtle Anatomy of Man.* 1972. Reprint. Essex, England: Health Science Press, 1980.

Thera, N. *The Heart of Buddhist Meditation.* 1962. Reprint. York Beach, ME: Samuel Weiser, 1973.

Tyberg, J. M. *The Language of the Gods.* Los Angeles: East-West Cultural Centre, 1970.

White, J., and S. Krippner, eds. *Future Science.* Garden City, NY: Anchor-Doubleday, 1977.

Yukteswar, Swami. *The Holy Science.* 1949. Reprint. Los Angeles: Self-Realization Fellowship, 1977.